DIARY

OF

A JOURNEY ACROSS ARABIA

FROM EL KHATIF IN THE PERSIAN GULF,
TO YAMBO IN THE RED SEA, DURING THE YEAR 1819.

(WITH A MAP.)

BY

Captain G. FORSTER SADLIER,

OF H. M's. 47th REGIMENT.

COMPILED FROM THE RECORDS OF THE BOMBAY GOVERNMENT.

BY

P. RYAN, Esq.,

ASSISTANT SECRETARY TO GOVERNMENT.

Bombay:
PRINTED AT THE
EDUCATION SOCIETY'S PRESS, BYCULLA.

1866.

TABLE OF CONTENTS.

	PAGE
Introduction	i—iii
Remarks on the Route	1—4
Diary	4—128
Appendices—	
Instructions	129—137
A	138—150
B	151—158

INTRODUCTION.

The following pages contain a narrative of a journey performed nearly half a century ago by Captain G. Forster Sadlier, of the British Army, across the peninsula of Arabia, a region which has recently been invested with an unusual degree of interest by the revelations of Mr. Gifford Palgrave.

Captain Sadlier was appointed by the Bombay Government in 1819 to proceed on a mission to the Camp of Ibrahim Pacha, who was at that time engaged in the subversion of the Wahabee Power in Arabia.

The object* of his mission was briefly to congratulate the Pacha on his successes against the Wahabees, which had lately resulted in the capture of their capital town of Deriah, and to ascertain how far he might be inclined to coöperate with the British Government in the reduction of the Wahabee pirates in the Persian Gulf.

As the exact position of the Pacha's camp was not known to the Bombay Government, Captain Sadlier was directed to call in the first place at Muscat for the purpose of communicating with the Imam on the intended expedition against the piratical tribes in the Persian Gulf, and of obtaining information regarding the route by which he might proceed to his destination.

Instead of finding the Pacha of Egypt on the shores of the Persian Gulf, and passing the period of his mission in the Turkish Camp in communication with a British Force, Captain Sadlier was compelled to perform an arduous journey of twelve

---

* A copy of the instructions furnished to Captain Sadlier will be found in the Appendix.

hundred miles across the deserts of Arabia from Katif in the Persian Gulf by Lahissa to Yambo in the Red Sea—an enterprise never before attempted by any European.

In 1821 the Literary Society of Bombay, in publishing an account of this extraordinary journey, observed :—

"Travelling, however, expeditiously and alone, through a country in which the exact position of a single town has never been ascertained, and unprovided with the necessary instruments, it has not been in Captain Sadlier's power to give that geographical precision to his route which he would have wished; but he was particularly attentive in frequently marking the direction of his march by a very good compass, and in noting exactly the time of each day's journey; and by such means, as it is well known, a near approximation to the truth may be obtained.

"The principal part of Captain Sadlier's journey lay through the provinces of Hajar, or Bahrein, and Najd, which have been always the residence of the Bedouin tribes. Their peculiar mode of life, and the deserts which they inhabit, must ever prevent any material change taking place in their manners, customs, and government. Hence the accurate description of them given by Niebuhr fifty-eight years ago will be found equally correct at this day. He observes with regard to Hajar: 'Tout le district appartient à la tribu Beni Káled, une des plus puissantes parmi les Arabes, laquelle s'étend si avant dans le désert qu'elle inquiète souvent les caravans entre Bagdad et Halel. Le Shech anjourd'hui regnant se nomme Arär. La plus grande partie de ce pays est habitée par les Bédouins, et par diverses tribus qui reconnaissent la souveraineté de la tribu Beni Khaled. On y trouve encore plusieurs villes. Lachsa est la résidence du Shech regnant.'* Captain Sadlier mentions that Lahissa, Katif, and the greatest part of this district had been reduced by the Turks; and that on Ibrahim Pacha withdrawing his troops from this part of Arabia, Lahissa and its dependencies were restored to the Beni Khalid,

---

* Niebuhr, *Description de l'Arabie*, p. 294.

INTRODUCTION.

but as tributaries to the Pacha, who claimed a proportion of the revenues as a remuneration for the expenses of the war, and for re-instating the tribe in their former possessions. Niebuhr concludes his account of the sea-ports of this province by observing, 'Je ne sais, au reste, aucune particularité des autres villes et villages de l'intérieur du pays.'* On this point Captain Sadlier's Journal will afford new and important information."

Very little can be gleaned from the records of the Bombay Government regarding Captain Sadlier's public career. He was an officer of H. M.'s 47th Regiment, and was introduced to the notice of Sir Evan Nepean, Governor of Bombay, by Lord Hastings, to whom he had commended himself while employed in Persia. The successful manner in which he carried out his mission to Ibrahim Pacha induced the Honourable Mr. Elphinstone, on Captain Sadlier's return from Arabia in 1820, to entrust him with a mission to the Ameers of Sind, who had about that time evinced a desire to improve their relations with the British Government. Captain Sadlier returned from Sind in May 1821, and rejoined his Regiment in India, with which he appears to have proceeded eventually to England in 1825.

---

* Id. Ibid.

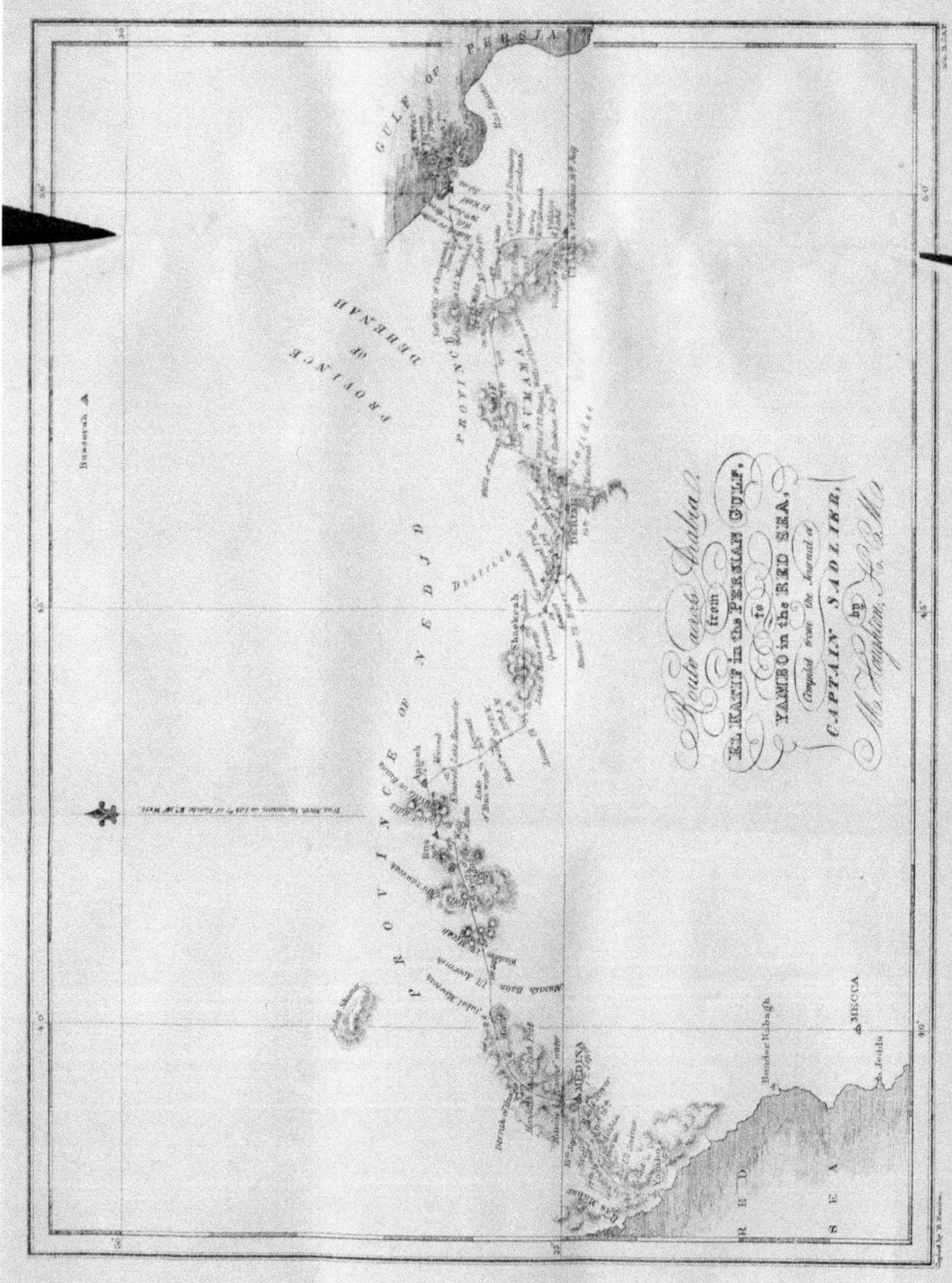

REMARKS

ON THE

ROUTE ACROSS ARABIA,

FROM

EL-KATIF IN THE PERSIAN GULF

TO

YAMBO IN THE RED SEA.

With a view to elucidate the general direction of my route, to mark the probable relative positions of the intervening towns or places which I passed in this journey, and to render the narrative of His Excellency Ibrahim Pacha's exploits more clear, I have affixed a route across Arabia from Katif to Yambo.

During the first stages I was obliged to guess at the distances, not being as yet sufficiently acquainted with the pace and gait of the camel to form an idea of the rate at which we were moving; a few days' observation and timing the animal's pace enabled me to form a tolerably correct opinion, and thence deduce a rate for my general guidance, by calculating from the number of hours we were actually on the march.

For marches not exceeding eight hours I calculated three miles an hour, and for marches exceeding that number of hours I lessened the computed distance to two and half and to two and three-quarter miles per hour, making a deduction in some cases for hilly and rocky ground.

The general direction of the line of march I took frequently with a very good compass, always alighting from my camel, its motion being too rough to admit of a compass being used even when in a walk.

From Katif we proceeded by broken stages to Oomerrubeeah in the desert, and thence by a retrograde and circuitous route to Ul Ahsa,* from whence we returned very unexpectedly to Oomerrubeeah by a different route. On laying down the track thus far there does not appear to be any considerable error, as the distances and bearings which I had taken brought me within seven or eight miles of my first calculation.

From this point we again set out with the intention of proceeding direct to Deriah, but an unlucky event obliged this route to be abandoned, and we again became wanderers in the desert till we reached Munfooah and Riaz, to the south of Deriah. These were the only settled habitations of man which we had met with for fourteen days from the period of our departure from Ul-Ahsa.

From the site of Deriah we proceeded towards Anizeh, one of the principal towns in the interior of Arabia. I frequently inquired of the guides and Bedouins who accompanied us how many marches and what towns intervened, and was a good deal surprised when they all agreed that we should pass through Shakra before we would reach Anizeh. The position of these two places with regard to Deriah appears to me to be reversed on the printed maps.

Quitting Shakra we eventually arrived at Anizeh and Rus, from whence I reluctantly set off for the Holy City of Medina, which I have placed according to the latitude and longitude assigned to it in the new maps of 1819. Although my calculations did not bring me so far south, I have allowed for the variation of the compass during this westerly course, as it appears to be considerable in the latitude of Yambo, being nearly one point.

An unlucky accident which occurred near Medina precluded the possibility of my making any just observations on the mazy windings of our route through the extraordinary valley, which affords

---

* Ul Ahsa, Lahsa, or Lahissa is properly the name of a district, and not of any particular town, as will appear in the description of that tract of country, but as Arrowsmith, Pinkerton, &c., still continue to mark the principal town by that name, I have conformed to them.

a communication or passage through the range of mountains which separates Ul Hejanj from Nedjed. This valley is very confined, and our caravan was much too numerous to proceed in one body. I do not imagine that we exceeded two miles an hour during this part of the journey.

I have inserted the names of many places that do not appear on any printed map of Arabia, but I have limited the insertion to those only through which I passed myself, many of which are mentioned in the narrative of His Excellency's campaign against the Wahabees.

On comparing this route with the maps of Arabia now in print, the positions I have assigned to many places will be found to differ from some of them materially. I have already noticed Shakra, and had I in this instance adhered to the maps, the position of that place would have been much too far to the north for the theatre of His Excellency's exploits, from the narrative of which it is evident that Shakra must have lain in his route as an impediment to his approach to Deriah subsequent to the fall of Rus, Anizeh, &c. If Shakra had been situated at the foot of Jubul Chummer, as Pinkerton has placed it, the Pacha must have visited it when he made the expedition to that place from Heneekah, and this occurred previous to the battle of Jubal Mawuch.

Mr. Pinkerton lays down Medina further to the south than Arrowsmith or Leake, and all the geographers differ from each other in the latitudes as well as the longitudes they assign to the places they mention in the interior of this part of Arabia.

This induces me to imagine that the maps have been compiled from the reports of Bedouins, and that the precise situations of those places have never been ascertained with mathematical precision. These Bedouins are very inexpert in tracing the relative position and distances of places. They have no fixed measurement to compute their distances, such as miles, coss, farsungs; and their general method of estimating time is by days' marches. The rising sun points out the east, and the setting the west, or the direction of Mecca. The north star and some others are known to the more intelligent Arabs, but in general they do not possess the same acuteness that the Indian Hurkarehs are so justly celebrated for. I have therefore confined myself in the present instance to my own observations.

From a route through a country in which the exact position of a single town has never been ascertained, precision will not, I hope, be expected, particularly when the very limited means at my disposal are taken into consideration, together with the insulated, solitary situation in which I very unexpectedly found myself.

DIARY.

1819, *April 14th*.—On the morning of the 14th April I received the instructions for the guidance of my conduct on this mission which had been prepared by order of the Right Honourable Sir Evan Nepean, Bart., Governor of Bombay, and embarked on the Honourable Company's cruizer "Thetis," commanded by Captain Tanner, this vessel being particularly ordered for this duty. The Commander received instructions to proceed in the first instance to Muscat, to enable me to communicate with the Imam; we therefore prepared to sail without further delay. My hopes, however, of a speedy passage were much damped by the advanced season of the year, which rather led us to anticipate a tedious voyage.

The "Thetis," although a brig of war, mounting 14 guns, was ill adapted, from her build, for sailing, and of so small a class, that little room could be appropriated to the conveyance of baggage. I therefore obtained permission to send the tents which had been furnished for my use to Bushire by a merchant vessel proceeding to that place, and this proved rather a lucky arrangement, as the "Thetis" could not possiby have received them. Even the presents with which I had been provided were stowed in the boat on deck.

April 16th.—On the evening of the 16th April we fell in with H. M.'s ship "Conway," from the Gulf. My anxiety to obtain information from that quarter induced me to accompany Lieut. Tanner, who proceeded on board to pay a visit to Captain Barnard, from whom we learned that there had not been a depredation committed by the Joassmees within the Gulf for many months, although the complaints of the cruelties committed by them in other quarters were very numerous. He had met with an empty boat at sea the day previous, which he supposed to have been plundered by the pirates. As Doctor Colquhoun (the late Resident at Bussorah) was a passenger in this ship, I mentioned the purport of my journey. He informed me that about six months ago the caravans were in the habit of passing frequently between Bussorah and the Turkish camp, but that latterly the communication was interrupted in consequence of a misunderstanding between Ibrahim Pacha and some of the Arab tribes. However, he stated that the communication between Bushire and Kuteef was in general open, and that by this route he conceived it easier to approach the Turkish army than by the Bussorah route. With respect to the Bahreinees he was not aware of any alteration having taken place.

May 4th.—The sameness of the voyage was broken through on the afternoon of the 4th of May by the discovery of land at a considerable distance. It was not, however, till the evening of 5th that we could discern it plainly. It became equally evident to us from another cause that we were within the Gulf. The thermometer, which hitherto had not risen above 85°, was now rising to 90 and soon reached 92°; we were evidently within Rus-ul-Hud.

May 7th.—On the morning of 7th May we were to the northwest of Cape Coriatte, the weather extremely sultry, and the wind baffling and light, the vessel moved slow, gradually approaching the stupendous mountains which overhang Muscat. In the evening we came to an anchor in the cove, and a boat was sent on shore to acquaint the Imam of the arrival of the cruizer on this station, and of the Commander's intention to salute the Fort. I availed myself of this opportunity to present my respects to His Highness through Lieutenant Nish, who proceeded in the boat. On his return the salute was fired, and answered by an equal number of guns from a fort, which was so much shook by the concussion that a part of the parapet gave way and rolled into the sea.

The observance of this necessary etiquette was productive of a most serious loss to me in my present situation: my thermometer, which had hung in the cabin during the voyage in a wooden case covered with leather, was broken into so many minute particles that it became difficult to separate the glass from the quicksilver with which it was intermixed in the bottom of the case. At Muscat it was totally impossible to procure another, and I could scarcely expect to supply myself with one in the Gulf of Persia.

As it would require several days to accomplish the object of my visit to Muscat, and as I was desirous to be in a situation of easy access to any persons from whom I could derive information, I requested the Imam to accommodate me with a house on shore for a few days. This was absolutely necessary, as the difficulty of going off to a small ship at unexpected hours would have been attended with inconvenience to all parties, and although a residence on shore was likely to be attended with unpleasant consequences to myself, I determined to sacrifice my personal or private convenience to the motives above mentioned.

May 8th.—I had the pleasure to receive a visit afloat from His Highness's Minister on the morning of the 8th, when it was arranged that I should be received at 11 o'clock, and then present the letter which had been entrusted to my charge by the Right Honourable the Governor of Bombay. The Minister appeared to be rather a stupid, drowsy man; a few fulsome compliments passed, and as there is but little etiquette observed at His Highness's court, the preliminaries of the presentation were easily arranged. The only request on his part was that I would not enter on business at the first interview.

H. M.'s sloop "Curlew," commanded by Captain Walpole, arrived early this morning, although she did not depart from Bombay till ten days subsequent to the "Thetis." On my way to the shore I paid a visit to Captain Walpole, who accompanied me in the "Thetis's" boat with Lieutenant Tanner. We were received on landing by the Minister, who conducted us to the Imam's palace, where His Highness and his brother were seated in a verandah at the end of a terrace, from whence the shipping in the cove were to be seen to advantage. The room was neatly carpeted, and furnished with chairs. Our reception was courteous. His Highness's inquiries after the health of each gentleman were expressed with much affability; after which he introduced his brother, Seyud Salem, and the Minister Sheikh Alee bin Fazil. His Excellency expressed the high sense he entertained of the friendly alliance and good understanding which has uniformly existed between the Honourable Company's Government and his family, and from which he has derived such constant support. Having replied to his inquiries respecting the health of the Right Honourable the Governor of Bombay, I approached for the purpose of presenting the letter which had been entrusted to my charge, on which His Highness arose from his chair, and received the letter with every appearance of satisfaction. The conversation which ensued was a complimentary inquiry respecting the late successes of the British arms in India and the expression of a perfect confidence in the result of the intended operations in the Persian Gulf. One subject was repeatedly urged, that the friends of each State were reciprocally considered as friends, and that the enemies of either would of course be considered as such by the other; this evidently had an allusion to some topic as yet in embryo. The visit having been protracted to an unusual length, we withdrew, and retired to the smoky habitation in which I was to take up my quarters during my stay at Muscat.

His Highness's Minister waited on me in the evening and entered into a long discussion, which was intended as a prelude to inquiries respecting my journey to Deriah, the advance of the Turkish army on the coast of the Red Sea, and the proximity of the scene of action contemplated on the coast of the Persian Gulf to the boundary of the Imam's dominions, were no doubt events to which the Imam would look with extreme jealousy; it required much argument to induce the Minister to depart with an apparent degree of satisfaction, although I could not perceive that he was much interested in the result. He appeared to be rather a lethargic man, advanced in years, with more than an usual portion of apathy blended in his disposition even as an Arab. Having evinced every possible desire to afford His Highness leisure to peruse the letter which I had presented, and to await his leisure to enter on the arrangements alluded to in that address, I however thought it was also necessary to prevent the probable inconveniences arising from delay at this advanced season of the year, and therefore urged my desire to wait on the Imam, if possible, on the following day.

May 9th.—On the morning of the 9th I expected to be summoned to attend, but the Minister appeared with a budget of news respecting the fall of Brimee, and the expected arrival of Buttal Wahabee, the late chief of that district. Although good news were rather seldom promulgated at Muscat, I must confess that I listened to this long communication with some degree of impatience. Nearly a whole day passed in learning that the dissensions between some of the Chiefs of the Joassmees had induced this Sheikh to throw himself on the mercy of the Imam, in preference to resigning his power to the Chiefs of Shargah and Aieman, who in all probability would have deprived him of his head to make room for one of their own adherents. Brimee is described to be a very strong fort with two bastions or towers, built of masonry, surrounded by a very deep ditch. The distance from Ras-ul-Khima and Shargah to Brimee is stated to be two days' march, inland; this place had afforded succours to Ras-ul-Khima, and from the country in its neighbourhood reinforcements of cavalry, camels, &c., were generally despatched whenever the latter place was threatened. The Minister prolonged his account of the warfare, which he said had taken place, with a view, no doubt, to impress on my mind the prowess of the troops which had been sent against Buttal, who, I believe, yielded to the policy of the times, and not to the bravery of His Highness's troops.

In the evening of the 9th I obtained my second interview, when I found the Imam and the Minister seated as usual in the verandah; they appeared in a very gloomy mood, and I found it extremely difficult to agitate or introduce the motives of my visit to Muscat. His Highness expressed himself with much vehemence whenever he had occasion to introduce the name of the Pacha. All my efforts to draw his attention to other topics were vain, and I found myself obliged to argue the point with much more warmth than I had been led to expect. He expatiated on the impossibility of my getting to Deriah, or being able to return from thence (should I fortunately reach the camp) in time to make any arrangements in which the Pacha could be connected, even was he at liberty to enter into our views without consulting the Pacha of Egypt. He reviled the conduct of Ibrahim Pacha, and charged him with acts of cruelty against the Arabs, the reports of which would prevent him from being able to associate his Arab troops with the Pacha's Turks. Having allowed His Highness to vent a portion of his mighty anger, I was obliged to urge my arguments in reply, and after a long conference it was agreed that His Highness's troops were not to be expected to act in conjunction with the Turks—a point which in reality (like many others at issue) never could be required if the Turkish army should appear on the stage. The principal object that the Imam had in view was of course to preclude the introduction of the Turkish army, but as he could not substitute an equivalent, this point could not be acquiesced in. He then naturally turned his thoughts to forming a barrier against the future encroachments of Ibrahim Pacha, and expressed his hopes that he would find the British Government ready to support his cause, and frequently asked me to give him a pledge to that effect, my reply to which was invariably that the good understanding which has hitherto existed between Mahomed Ali Pacha and the British Government must be considered as the best pledge that can be offered for the future good understanding which the British Government expects and hopes to see established between Ibrahim Pacha and His Highness; that as hitherto no acts of

Ibrahim Pacha's conduct towards His Highness could be considered inimical, it would be indelicate to enter upon any measures anticipating such an improbable event. Our deliberations having been prolonged to a very unusual and unnecessary length, without having as yet canvassed any point which could tend to the completion of the enterprise, I was obliged to urge the necessity of His Highness evincing his inclination and determination to support the views of the British Government with all his resources, as upon this would depend in a great measure both the safety of His Highness's dominions from the encroachments of the Joassmees, and our countenance, in the event of any unlooked-for or unexpected alteration in the conduct of Ibrahim Pacha. To this His Highness replied by the most solemn assurances of his intention to assist the British Government in the reduction of the Joassmee pirates, adding that it was then too late an hour to enter into the details of the arrangements, but that he would be fully prepared to reply to any inquiries respecting their force, and the resources which he himself possesses, if I would attend at an early hour on the following day. I therefore withdrew, most heartily tired of long arguments, which as yet had been productive of so little satisfaction.

May 10*th*.—On the morning of the 10th I had the pleasure to receive a message from the Minister in reply to a communication which I had made to him. He informed me that His Highness had fully reconsidered the conversations of yesterday, and that I would find little difficulty in entering into the necessary arrangements. We therefore proceeded to His Highness's palace, where we found his brother seated with him.

The first point to be inquired into was the present state of the power of the Joassmees, and to my inquiries on this head, His Highness represented their power to be on the decline since the overthrow of the Wahabee Chiefs, which had given rise to the want of confidence in the different Joassmee Chiefs towards each other, or rather the conviction of the determination of each individual to attempt the advancement of his own interests at the expense of his neighbours'. This state of things he conceives to be very favourable ; the want of a leader of talent, and the present confined and cramped state of the Joassmees since the overthrow of the Wahabee power may probably breed dissensions among them. Very few of the Wahabees who have escaped from Deriah have joined the Joassmees, he does not estimate their number at more than three hundred. The following estimate of the whole force of the Joassmees, as they now exist, he had collected from the very best authority, and considers it as authentic :—

					Footmen.
* Joined from the remains of the Wahabee force, say					300
1. Bukha contains only					20
2. Shaam					150 to 200
3. Rums					200
4. Ras-ul-Khima, large boats 25, small 75, and					300
5. Humrah, all joined at Ras-ul-Khima.					
6. Oom-ul-Goweyn	,,	1	,, 30	,,	400
7. Ajmaan	,,	4	,, 35	,,	1,000
8. Fusht, with	} ,,	12	,, 150	,,	1,280
9. Shargeh					
10. Aboo Heyle, in the foregoing.					
11. Dubyee	,,	4	,, 100	,,	800
		46	,, 390	,,	7,200
Boo Dubyee, Khyram Buneeyas	,,	5	,, 300	,,	3,000

This last port can scarcely be considered as a piratical port, having been long disunited from Ras-ul-Khima.

To the east of cape Mussendom is the small bay of Fuggeerah, which serves as a look-out post on this side for boats coming up the Gulf from Fuggeerah or from Dubah. An Arab causid can pass the mountains to Ras-ul-Khima in fourteen hours; the road

---

* This part of the force of Ras-ul-Khima had been at one period exaggerated to fifteen thousand men ; it appears that Leif bin Sadoon brought with him 200 men determined ; Leeah Sub Abdool bin Muzuroo had only 50 followers ; and Bin Abdan 50, making a total of 300. I have never heard the names of any others mentioned.

from Dubah is passable for foot and horse and even for small guns, and the journey can be effected in two days.

The present disposition of the Shargeh Chief may probably induce him as well as the Chief of Ajmaan to remain disunited from the Chief of Ras-ul-Khima pending the hostilities. His Highness has therefore declared his intention to use his endeavours to effect this object, although he recommends the whole to meet with the same fate that may attend Ras-ul-Khima.

I therefore proposed to His Highness that we should take into consideration the measures to be adopted in the offensive operations. After some circumlocution and argument, His Highness agreed to the following arrangements, which he requested me to commit to writing, and to transmit in reply to that part of my instructions touching the nature and extent of the assistance he may be able to afford in the reduction of the piratical ports :—

With a view to preventing the fugitive Joassmees of Ras-ul-Khima from entering into Oman, His Highness intends to post a sufficient number of men in the passes of the mountains, pending the operations against Ras-ul-Khima, should the services of those men not be required in consequence of the arrival of the Pacha's army, but if that event does not take place, His Highness will be prepared to coöperate by land with a force of seven thousand foot, one hundred and thirty horse, and fifteen hundred camels, to proceed by the passes above Ras-ul-Khima, and invest that place. He himself will accompany the expedition in a ship of war, and take with him at least one thousand men, to be landed, and to act in conjunction with the British force, it being understood that if Ibrahim Pacha's force acts by land, the Imam's force will all proceed by sea, except that part required for the purpose already stated, of guarding the passes into Oman. The necessary precautions will of course be taken to prevent the Arab and Turkish soldiery being employed in conjunction with each other, and their camps shall be at all times separate.

The next assistance to be afforded on his part appeared to be the supply of boats to assist in the disembarkation of troops, baggage, &c. Unfortunately the number of boats of the description required for that purpose is much diminished within these few years. His Highness stated that he could not promise a greater number than seventy, but if possible he would increase the number to one hundred, each capable of conveying from thirty to fifty men.

With respect to water and firewood, His Highness stated that a sufficiency of each should be supplied at His Highness's expense, but that cattle, and such other supplies as were necessary, would be procured more readily by our own commissary, who would pay only the regulated price, His Highness exerting his influence to prevent overcharge.

His Highness consents to employ two of his ships for the conveyance of stores, or in whatever way they may be best applied, agreeable to the wishes of the British Government, at whose disposal two ships will be placed whenever the Right Honourable the Governor in Council may intimate his wishes on that subject to His Highness.

His Highness will keep up a correspondence with the Government of Bombay on all subjects connected with the advancement of the preparations for the expedition, and will forward every information that he may obtain relative to any alterations that may take place in the force or number of the Joassmee pirates, so that the Government may at all times be perfectly acquainted with the actual state of their power.

His Highness concluded with a general assurance of support and assistance, and stated that any measures adopted by the British Government should meet with his warmest support; that, independent of the particulars here enumerated, he would be happy to forward the views of Government by attending to any arrangements that may have been omitted in the foregoing outline.

It is very obvious that the introduction of Ibrahim Pacha's force, and the proximity of the scene of action to the boundary of His Highness's territory, are two subjects which give rise to feelings of jealousy and suspicion in the mind of the Imam, particularly when it is recollected that the Pacha's views towards obtaining possession of Bahrein have become public, and that he has not satisfied the Imam's inquiries on that subject. The Imam therefore, in the first instance, appears to have had in view the possibility of inducing me to give up the idea of proceeding to Deriah, first arguing the distance and delay, next the possibility of effecting the overthrow of the Joassmees without the assistance of the Pacha. Not having carried this point, he next assayed to obtain a pledge from me on the part of the British Government, but to this I invariably replied by repeating that part of the letter addressed by the Right Honourable the Governor in Council to His Highness, and on no occasion did I exceed the limits of the assurances conveyed in that address.

From the information I have collected here from other sources, I do not imagine that the Imam has underrated the forces of the Joassmees, neither can I learn from any authority on which I could depend that the Arabs of the interior will come forward to assist the Joassmees of Ras-ul-Khima. If they were inclined to join their former associates, the number of men they could bring into the field would not exceed three thousand, and if the Brimee Chief and his associates can be depended upon, even that number would be considerably diminished. It appears that the Imam's force amounts to twenty thousand foot-men, distributed throughout the villages and along the coast of Oman; but although every Arab is a soldier, and armed, it is not to be supposed that the army is disposable. Of the twenty thousand foot, it is probable ten thousand may be collected at one point, and of his cavalry not more than one hundred and thirty or one hundred and fifty.

Having thus far concluded the deliberations on the subject of the preparations, and assistance which His Highness would be enabled to set on foot, I expected to be able to depart from Muscat in the course of a few days, but the melancholy occurrence of the demise of a relative of His Highness's family rendered a delay of some days necessary, to afford leisure for His Highness to prepare his despatch in reply to the communication which I had the honour to present from the Right Honourable the Governor in Council of Bombay, and as the principal objection which had arisen in the course of our conferences was of that delicate nature to preclude its being introduced in a public document from the Imam, it became necessary to enter into some arrangement which would authenticate the assurances which His Highness had made to me, without introducing the name of the third party. I therefore drew up the memorandum of those assurances, and the particulars stated in them, to which His Highness assented, and stated, " that in his letter he would refer to the communication which he authorised me to make on these heads, and authenticate these promises by stating them to be correctly reported." The tenor of my instructions and of the letter addressed to the Imam did not authorize me to require a more critical or a more formal reply to the communication with the delivery of which I had been charged.

Addressed a letter* to the Right Honourable Sir Evan Nepean, Bart., President and Governor in Council, Bombay, in which I fully detailed the whole of the foregoing.

On the 13th Lieutenant Tanner officially reported the "Thetis" to be in readiness to proceed on the further prosecution of the voyage, and as he required an official reply, I of course addressed a letter to that gentleman, although such a communication was in reality unnecessary, as the subject had been most fully canvassed; indeed it would appear self-evident that I could proceed only by the route of Kateef, and that this harbour could not be entered in a square-rigged vessel without taking the precaution of having a native pilot on board. As such a man would more conveniently be procured at Bushire, where the camp equipage for my use had been forwarded to, I had no hesitation in determining to proceed to Bushire, where I would obtain every requisite information respecting the situation of the Pacha's camp. My departure from Muscat could only depend on the will and pleasure of the Imam, whose reply I awaited.

---

* This letter was received at Bombay in May 1819, and a copy forwarded to Calcutta. (*Vide* Appendix A.)

In the afternoon I availed myself of the leisure afforded to pay a visit to Seyud Salim, His Highness's brother, by whom I was received with every mark of politeness and regard. As the Seyud had resided at Shiraz for some months, he considered it necessary to show that he had been a traveller, and introduced fruits and sherbets after the Persian custom. Smoking being interdicted to the Sheikhs or Chiefs of the tribe or sect of Beiasi, this latter part of the ceremony of a Persian visit could not be complied with. I observed that the doors of the hall were closed when the refreshments were served up, and an inclination to secrecy was evidently evinced. This impressed me with an idea that the Seyud did not wish it to appear publicly that he ate off the same board with an infidel; the fruits were laid on a table, but I did not perceive that any of the company were at all scrupulous of eating off the same dish, or using the same bowl out of which I had tasted. On my return from this visit I called on the Minister, who treated me with coffee, but even here smoking formed no part of the entertainment of the visit. The etiquette of visiting is on the whole much more rudely conducted among the Arabs than with the Persians.

On the afternoon of the 14th His Highness intimated to me his intention of honouring me with a visit of ceremony, and although my smoky habitation was ill adapted for the reception of His Highness, I was obliged to receive this mark of condescension in the best apartment which the sooty and tottering fabric afforded. The Imam's manner is plain, and his deportment courteous. He appears to be blessed with a good temper and disposition, and seldom displays peevishness, except under the vulgar irritation of business, to which he is not unfrequently exposed, as he generally transacts even trifling affairs himself. During this visit he appeared perfectly at his ease, which I was cautious not to interrupt by the intrusion of business, or even by expressing my anxiety at the delay which I was obliged to endure. On departing His Highness apologized for the badness of the accommodation which Muscat afforded, and promised to enable me to depart, if possible, on the Sunday following. This was joyful news, as my servants had suffered severely from indisposition, proceeding no doubt from the insalubrity of the climate, as well as from the inconveniences to which they were exposed. I therefore sent on board those who had been attacked with fever, and prepared to embark on the following day.

May 15*th*.—The arrival of H. M.'s ship "Eden," commanded by Captain Lock, on the morning of 15th, afforded me the opportunity of communicating with that officer. As he had heard some reports in circulation at Bushire relative to Ibrahim Pacha's treasure and convoys having been plundered by the Bedouins, and surmises as to the success of the detachments which had been sent in pursuit, I thought it prudent not to accompany Captain Lock on his visit to the Imam, who, however, abstained from any remarks connected with the subject of my mission to Muscat.

Having consulted with Captain Lock on the propriety of my proceeding to Bushire in the first instance, I was pleased to find that his opinion so perfectly coincided with the resolution I had formed on the 13th instant.

His Highness's Secretary informed me that the letters would be prepared by the afternoon. I therefore proposed to make a farewell visit to the Imam, who received me in the evening, and delivered the letters in duplicate, the one being closed in a Khinkhab bag, agreeable to etiquette, the other copy open, as it contained an authority for my proceedings in the execution of my mission to Muscat. On this occasion the assurances of concert and assistance were repeated by His Highness, and on my part I availed myself of the opportunity to introduce a subject which may possibly smooth the way to the accomplishment of our undertaking. As the situation of Muscat is considered extremely unhealthy, and its contiguity affords an easy access to spies, I had long considered the advantage to be derived from forming a depôt for our troops on some one of the islands better situated, where the whole may rendezvous, and thence proceed direct to the point of attack. His Highness assured me that such a measure would meet with his approbation, and that he would even extend this privilege to any part of the troops composing the expedition, which from circumstances that may hereafter arise, it may appear politic to retain in the Gulf of Persia.

The foregoing conversation gave rise to the discussion of the question of tenure, or right, by which lands or territory may be defined, or considered to be hereditary sovereignty or feudal tenure, and on the subject the following conclusions were acquiesced in :—

The island of Kishm was recovered by Seyud Sultan from the tribe of Bin Miheenee, under the government of Moola Hassun, in the reign of Agha Mahomed Khan Kadjar, and has descended to the present Imam by the right of conquest, and over which His Highness extends the protection of a sovereign. No part whatever of the revenues of Kishm at the present moment reverts to any other sovereign, neither has any part of the revenue reverted to or been paid to any other power during or since the reign of Seyud Sultan.

Gomberoom Miana and Khumeer are held by virtue of a firman from the present king of Persia, for payment of the annual sum of tumans three thousand, and on a late occasion, when the Minister of Finance was desirous to increase the king's revenue, he required the Imam to pay an advance of one thousand tumans, stating that "if the Imam of Muscat would not give the sum, he would soon find another purchaser;" but no claim was made on Kishm, nor does the name of this place appear in that firman.

On the afternoon of 15th I embarked on the "Thetis." At noon 16th His Highness's Minister, accompanied by the broker, waited on me to present three Teermah shawls, which His Highness requested me to accept, offering his best wishes for the success of my journey, and assuring me he would be most happy to see me on my return. In accepting this mark of His Highness's entire satisfaction, I returned a complimentary message, wishing His Highness every success during his intended cruise in his new frigate, and presented a suitable donation to the servants who were the bearers of the shawls, which have been added to the stock of public presents.

Agreeable to a new arrangement made by Captain Lock, I transhipped to the "Mercury." Captain Lock sailed for Bombay at sunset, and His Highness the Imam sailed in his new frigate to cruise off Ras-ul-Jibbul. I was obliged to remain a reluctant prisoner in Muscat Cove till the morning of 18th, when the "Mercury" was ready to proceed on the prosecution of her voyage to Aboosheer; and the "Teignmouth" and "Thetis" were despatched in consequence of the very alarming reports of a square-rigged vessel having been attacked by the pirates off Ras-ul-Hud.

Addressed the following letter:—

"To the Right Honourable Sir EVAN NEPEAN, Bart.,
President and Governor in Council, Bombay.

"RIGHT HONOURABLE SIR,

"I do myself the honour to acquaint your Honourable Board that at an interview which took place subsequent to the closing of my last despatch, I availed myself of an opportunity, which offered during the conversation, to ascertain how far His Highness the Imam would be inclined to sanction the landing of any part of the troops to be employed on the intended expedition on any of the islands or territories supposed to be under the sovereignty of His Highness. I am happy in acquainting your Honourable Board that such a measure will meet with the approbation and concurrence of the Imam, who informed me that he would feel happy in extending such a privilege to any part of the troops composing the expedition which, from circumstances that may hereafter arise, it may appear politic to retain in the Gulf of Persia. Your Honourable Board may possibly view an offer or proposal of this nature in a favourable light, as it may be attended with beneficial effects in enabling Government to select a place for the rendezvous of the troops possibly in some more eligible situation than the cove of Muscat.

"The foregoing conversation gave rise to the discussion of the question of tenure or right, by which lands or territory may be defined, or considered to be hereditary sovereignty or feudal tenure, and on this subject the following conclusions were acquiesced in :—

"The island of Kishm was recovered by Seyud Sultan from the tribe of Bin Miheenee under the government of Moola Hossun, in the reign of Agha Mahomed Khan Kadjar, and has descended to the present Imam by the right of conquest, and over which His Highness extends the protection of a sovereign. No part whatever of the revenues of Kishm at the present moment reverts to any other sovereign, neither has any part of the revenue reverted to or been paid to any other power during or since the reign of Seyud Sultan.

"The tenure of Gomberoom Miana and Khumeer is a tenure in fief held by virtue of a firman from the present king of Persia, the annual sum of tumans three thousand reverting to His Majesty; and on a late occasion when the Minister of Finance was desirous to increase the king's revenue, he required the Imam to pay an advance of one thousand tumans, stating ' that if the Imam of Muscat would not give the sum, he would soon find another purchaser ;' but no claim was made on Kishm, nor does the name of this place appear in that firman.

" I have the pleasure to acquaint your Honourable Board that in consequence of the communication between Fugeerah and Ras-ul-Khima having become precarious since the fall of Brimee, the Joassmee pirates have been dispossessed from the port of Fuggeerah. I have recommended this place to be garrisoned, as it is the only spot on this side the Cape that can afford a lurking hole to those wretches.

" Agreeably to that part of my instructions directing me to communicate and consult with the Naval Commander in the Gulf, I have had the pleasure to lay before Captain Lock a copy of my proceedings, and of all other information which has fallen under my observation since my arrival here. Captain Lock having conceived it necessary and advisable to the furtherance of the public service that I should proceed from hence on the H. C. C. "Mercury"

I have, in compliance, embarked on this vessel; this arrangement promises to expedite my arrival at Bushire, and I feel particularly obliged by the freedom of communication with which I have been honoured during the stay of the Senior Naval Officer at this port.

"I have the honour to be, &c.

"H. C. C. 'Mercury,' Muscat Cove,
17th May 1819."

June 7th.—The voyage from Muscat to Bushire was rendered particularly tedious even for this advanced season of the year. We encountered a severe north-west gale, which caused a very heavy sea, and after an unpleasant passage we reached Bushire roads on the afternoon of 7th June. I was extremely anxious to expedite my departure, and therefore landed immediately, that the vessel might be at liberty to proceed to Hallilah (a few miles down the coast,) to complete her supply of water. Of this necessary article we had but one day's supply when we reached our anchorage.

Addressed the following letter:—

"To the Right Honourable Sir EVAN NEPEAN, Bart.,
President and Governor in Council, Bombay.

"SIR,—I have the honour to report my arrival at Bushire on the afternoon of 7th instant, and to acquaint the Right Honourable the Governor in Council that it is probable my detention at this place will not exceed the time necessary for equipping the vessel after her voyage, which has been rendered uncommonly tedious, owing to the prevalence of north-west gales in the Gulf at this season of the year. I have been informed since my arrival that His Excellency Ibrahim Pacha purposes to perform the pilgrimage to Mecca immediately after the month of Ramazan, and that it is probable he will from thence return to Egypt. An officer has been appointed to whom, during His Excellency's absence, the management of the government will be entrusted. My arrival therefore previous to this change becomes a most serious object, and although the present advanced season of the year presents many difficulties, I nevertheless trust that I shall be able to accomplish this part of the task allotted to me. As it appears doubtful whether the port of Kateef or of Anjeer may be the most convenient of approach, that point has been referred to Captain Walpole for his decision.

" His Excellency has lately been obliged to make an excursion from Deriah in pursuit of some tribes of Bedouins, who had the audacity to attack his convoys conveying treasure. In this instance he has had the good fortune to recover the treasure that was plundered, and to chastise the perpetrators, which salutary chastisement it is hoped will prevent a recurrence of these insults, although it can hardly be expected that in the present situation of affairs his army can be entirely free from such annoyances, and as sufficient time has not elapsed for securing the tranquillity of these newly acquired provinces, the result of a repetition of such audacious attacks may give rise to much inconvenience, and prevent the Pacha from being enabled to enter into our views, by obliging His Excellency to employ a large portion of his troops in the execution of the very harassing duty of pursuing the Bedouins, who retire into the desert with the booty which they may plunder, and which, one time in ten, cannot be again rescued from their grasp.

"The revolt of many tribes of Bedouins has, in a great measure, deranged the resources of Ibrahim Pacha, and will of course cramp his movements, but I am happy to learn that these revolts are not to be attributed to any acts of cruelty countenanced by the Pacha. On the contrary he has pursued the wise policy of attaching to his interests the principal tribe of Binee Khalid, whose chief, Sheikh Arreur bin Sadoon, had been dispossessed by the Wahabee. The descendants of this tribe under Mahomed bin Arreur and Mujeed bin Arreur have lately been reinstated in their family dignities, and their properties restored. The recollection of the indignities suffered and the difference of religion renders this tribe the most implacable enemy to the sect of Wahabee and to all those who were adherents of Saood. Mujeed bin Arreur is at Lahissa, and his brother remains in the neighbourhood with his Bedouin tribe. To this may be attributed the present tranquil state of the district, which is guarded by a small force of Turks not exceeding five hundred men.

"As it will evidently become an object of the first importance that Government should be acquainted with the nature of my reception at the Turkish camp, and of the means the Pacha may have at his disposal to forward the object of combined operations, I have decided on taking with me a despatch boat for the purpose of forwarding the earliest intelligence on these subjects. As I cannot possibly foresee at the present moment the probable period of my return to the Presidency, which circumstance must depend on so many occurrences not within my control, that I conceive it advisable to use every precaution to enable the Government to judge of the possibility of His Excellency's being able to coöperate at so early a period as the Right Honourable the Governor may expect, and of the possibility of which I certainly entertain some doubts, as it appears that His Excellency will scarcely enter on such an undertaking without the concurrence of superior authority. I am further induced to express an opinion that the Turkish Government is not at the present instant sufficiently established in the possession of the newly acquired territory, to undertake any operations which may remove so large a portion of the troops to so great a distance as this enterprise would require.

"As Captain Bruce has had occasion to address a letter to the Right Honourable the Governor on the subject of the ports on the Persian coast, from whence the pirates of Ras-ul-Khima obtain such constant support, it is unnecessary for me to enter into any detail on this point, which affords but the one conclusion, that they have for a long time past identified themselves with the pirates of Ras-ul-Khima, and placed themselves in the situation of enemies to the British Government.

" I have the honour to be, &c.

"*Bushire, 9th June* 1819."

Addressed the following letter:—

"To the Right Honourable Sir EVAN NEPEAN, Bart.,
President and Governor in Council, Bombay.

"RIGHT HONOURABLE SIR,

"I do myself the honour to acquaint your Honourable Board that, in consequence of the difficulties I am likely to encounter in procuring funds by the medium of Bills to defray the very heavy expenses I shall be exposed to in prosecuting my journey through Arabia, I have been obliged to draw from Captain Bruce, Resident at Bushire, a large sum in such coins as will be best adapted to the currency of that country, and with a view of making a deposit of the same at Lahissa with the most respectable agent I can select.

"I have the honour to acquaint you that I have now granted a set of Bills on your Honourable Board in favour of Captain William Bruce, Resident, or order, for the sum of Rupees (13,000) thirteen thousand, to meet the disbursements of my mission, and which I have to request your Honourable Board will direct to be accepted and carried to the debit of the same.

"I have the honour to be, &c.

"*Bushire, 16th June* 1819."

June 16*th*.—An unfortunate accident occurred on the arrival of the vessel at the watering place: a second north-west gale set in, and she parted from both her anchors; this obliged her to run into Bushire to obtain the assistance of boats to weigh them, and, although I did not require quite so long a period to equip, I was detained till the afternoon of the 16th, when I embarked on the Honourable Company's cruiser "Vestal."

The "Vestal" had been nominated to replace the "Mercury" on the Arab coast, and therefore, now despatched to avoid the inconvenience of relieving. We sailed from Bushire roads on the afternoon of 16th, and made the land on the Arab coast at noon of 18th, expecting that little difficulty would be presented in entering the harbour of Kateef, but our disappointment was great when we discovered that the old stupid pilot was totally ignorant of the harbour, and brought up with all sail set on the edge of a sandbank, where we remained for the night, not being able to better our situation. I despatched Sheikh Khumees with a letter to the Turkish governor at Kateef, to request a pilot to take us to Anjeer, to which place I had been recommended to proceed, as being much nearer to Lahissa, and the best point for establishing a communication, and for this purpose I had hired a despatch boat at Bushire to accompany the cruiser, that I might have every facility of communicating. This Sheikh had offered his services as a guide, having resided for many months on this side, and made two journeys to Deriah; I therefore thought it advisable to have a person with me who would be personally known to the Bedouin Sheikhs.

The Sheikh did not return on the following morning, as I had anticipated, and, as a pilot could not be procured, every effort was tried to discover a channel up the southern side of the bay, without success. On the afternoon of 19th, Ruhman bin Jaber sent a boat to congratulate us on our arrival. I had been anxious to discover the haunt of this barbarian, which is on the southern side of the bay, and did not succeed till a few hours previous to the arrival of his boat on board the "Vestal." His man returned with a promise that a pilot should be sent in the boat I had despatched, and that no delay should take place. Sheikh Ruhman fulfilled his promise, and sent on board two intelligent pilots, who conducted the vessel with the morning's tide into the channel for ships, which is on the northern side, where there is a fine deep channel running close to and parallel with the narrow spit of sandy land by which this side of the bay is formed, or separated from the ocean. Here we anchored on the afternoon of 20th, having lost two days through the ignorance of the Bushire pilot, who certainly has no claim to confidence. To our inquiries respecting the harbour of Anjeer, Sheikh Ruhman replied that it would impossible to approach it in a large vessel, that a small vessel may lie off at a considerable distance, but that he would not undertake to go round Bahrein except during the day time, as the passage is intricate and rocky. Sheikh Khumees on his return brought the same information from Kateef. Khuleel Agha, the Turkish governor, so strongly recommended proceeding by the route of Kateef that I determined to give up the idea of reaching Anjeer by going round the southern bank of Bahrein, which would have required probably two days. I therefore landed on the morning of Monday, 21st, at the village of Seeahat, which is situated on the southern side of the bay, about three miles below Kateef.—Khuleel Agha had sent Eusoof Agha, an intelligent Turkish soldier, who officiated as collector of the customs, and next in dignity to himself, to accompany me from the ship, and pitched upon this spot for my residence, as he said the town or city was so very unhealthy that it would be dangerous for me to take up my residence in it even for a night; the distance from the anchorage to the landing place near the village was certainly twelve miles, and the spot where we landed, as well as the whole length of this beach, is so very shallow that camels and horses are used to convey persons from the boats; all baggage, &c., is brought off by camels or asses.

June 21*st*.—On the afternoon of 21st I was led to expect that I should have the honour to receive a visit from Khuleel Agha, and the report of some guns induced me to think that he was about to depart from the fort of Kateef. On the arrival of an Arab who brought a letter from the Agha, we learned that the guns were intended as a return to the salute fired by the "Vestal" in the morning, and that the Agha's health did not admit of his paying a visit this evening, which he, however, said he would be happy to do on the following morning, and requested that the doctor of the "Vestal" would afford him medical advice, which was of course offered, and a boat despatched to convey him on shore.

June 22nd.—Khuleel Agha did not make his appearance on the morning of 22nd, and as I was anxious to inquire respecting his health, I despatched my Meerza to pay him a visit, during which Mushruf-aal-ul-Arreeur, nephew of Muhmud bin Arreeur, who is the head of the tribe of Bennee Khaleed, waited on the Agha. This meeting was conducted with some degree of acrimony. The Arab stated publicly that the Turk who was placed here by Muhmud Agha Kashif (the Turkish governor of Lahissa) retained his authority contrary to the orders of the Pacha, and that he suppressed the orders issued to himself to place Mushruf in authority. The Turk, however, repelled the accusation, and declined complying with the demands of Mushruf, whom he directed to write to his uncle and require camels, horses, &c., and a guard to accompany me to Lahissa, whither he prepared to despatch a Causid to inform his superior of the steps he purposed to take. Khuleel Agha desired the Meerza to acquaint me that he was averse to my proceeding to Lahissa till he had received instructions, and that he did not conceive it prudent to place implicit confidence in the Bedouins.

Mushruf waited on me in the evening, and as I was desirous of forming an acquaintance, I accepted his polite offer of supplying me with cattle, and promised to meet his wishes with respect to the hire of the cattle, if necessary. On the return of the Causid he wished to impress me with the idea that his tribe could alone afford me the protection I required, and to this I replied by assuring him of my perfect confidence in his friendship. I wrote a letter to his uncle acquainting him with my arrival, and renewing the intercourse of friendship which had so long existed between his tribe and the gentlemen under the British Government who had heretofore been employed in this part of the world.

As I had requested the Agha to send horses early this morning, 23rd, to enable Doctor Bly to visit him, I waited the arrival of his messenger till twelve o'clock, at which hour he had not made his appearance; the doctor was of course obliged to return to the ship without prescribing a remedy for the Agha's complaint, which I understood was chiefly attributed to an edacious appetite.

June 24th.—On the morning of 24th I despatched the Sheikh to pay a visit to Khuleel Agha, and at the same time wrote him a complimentary letter, reminding him of my wish to depart for Lahissa the instant he could afford me the necessary protection. On this point the Sheikh was instructed to make some private inquiries. The Agha's temper, which is represented to be naturally morose, was much agitated by the news of his removal having become public. Mushruf-aal-ul-Arreeur had received orders to supply cattle to convey the governor's baggage and his two deputies to Lahissa, and to take charge of the government himself. Being desirous to be installed in his new dignity without delay, he appeared at the gate of the city with his suite of attendants, and was refused admission unless he chose to enter with only two of them; this he declined. During the altercation which took place through the medium of messengers, the Turk armed himself in his chamber, which resounded with his vociferations. Mushruf prudently retired, and the Turk applied himself to regulate his accounts, in which branch he appears to be an adept, converting tens into hundreds, and *vice versa*, with the greatest facility.

Although Khuleel Agha, the governor of Kateef, had despatched an express camelman to Lahissa, I conceived that by addressing a letter to Muhmud Agha Kashif, and sending it express, I might induce him to expedite my journey and departure from Lahissa. I therefore wrote a letter to that officer and sent it off express on the evening of 25th instant.

I shall attempt to give as correct a description of Kateef and the country in its neighbourhood as my imperfect observations will afford. The Bay of Kateef is nearly 20 miles in breadth at the entrance, formed by a very long narrow sandy neck on the northern, and by a flat sandy plain on the southern side; the northern point is called Rasut-ul-Noorah and the southern Zaheran. The island of Taroot lies in the centre and towards the top of the bay, being about ten miles in length, extending north-west and south-east, thickly planted with date trees, and well supplied with water. A bank projects from this island toward the opening of the bay in the form of a scollop shell and divides the bay into two channels; the northern, as before described, is deep and safe, running parallel and close to the sandy neck; the southern is shallow and intricate, being at a considerable distance from the shore, which is very flat, and between the channel and the shore very shallow; this side has one very peculiar mark—a sugar-loaf hill on the main, called Zaheran; further into harbour is a tower or fort called Dumam, surrounded by water, and lately repaired by Ruhman bin Jaber; above this is the village of Seehat on the main, and about four miles higher up the fort of Kateef, which is abreast of the island of Taroot.

The northern channel is the safest for ships, but is situated at a very considerable distance from Kateef; in getting from this anchorage to Kateef large boats are obliged to go round the bank of Taroot. This channel is very easy of access, as it only requires to accommodate the course to the form of the narrow sandy neck, keeping about a cable's length off shore, till you get abreast of Taroot, when two small sandy isles nearly at the top of the bay, and a decrease of water, give timely notice. Here a vessel is safe from north-western gales, but the bottom is sand.

The fort of Kateef has three gates, and is of an irregular oblong form; the longest face, towards the sea, having a citadel in the northernmost corner or angle, which is supplied by a good spring of water, and supposed to have been built by the Portuguese. There are some good houses within the fort; the depth of water at the landing place is greater than at Seehat, as before described, but even here very inconvenient. A market is held outside the south fort gate every Thursday, and a good supply of mutton, rice, dates, musk, and water-melons of an extraordinary size (some thirty-five to forty lbs.). Wheat and barley are not produced in as great abundance as rice, and to the cultivation of this latter is attributed the unhealthy air of Kateef. Figs are here abundant and tolerably good. Some apricots and a few mangoes, pomegranates, and grapes, citrons and limes are cultivated. The brinjal or badinjoon, onions, and beans are to be seen in the gardens, which extend to a considerable length, skirted by the desert on the one side and the sea-beach on the other, and shaded by plantations of date trees, interspersed with hamlets; the whole well supplied with water from wells, and although the soil is sandy, it is capable of producing large crops.

The trade of Kateef, now trifling, is carried on principally with Bahrein, through which goods from Surat, spices, sugars, &c. &c., from India, are supplied. Bahrein* is in fact the key to Bahran, Kateef and Anjeer being both supplied from that island; Lahissa and the interior being dependent for those supplies which reach the Bedouins through this channel. The consumption hitherto has been but trifling, owing to the unsettled state of the country, and the Bedouins having removed to the northward. Lahissa is supplied chiefly through Anjeer, as being a more direct communication; this of course diminishes the trade of Kateef.

I shall enumerate the towns or villages under the government of Kateef:—

	Population.
Kateef town	4,000
Suburbs of ditto	2,000
Taroot	2,400
Safwa	2,400
Awameeah	2,400
Liam	800
Jisha	560
Ummoolkman	1,600
Yaroodeah	1,200
Seehat	2,000

The above are walled towns.

---

* Bahrein is an island; the continent opposite is called Bahran.

The following open villages :—   Population.

Village	Population
Mullahah	400
Lugooah	400
Khoeldeah	1,600
Chés-il-Tobe	480
Chés-il-Bari	560
Hilutumheish	1,200
Debebi	1,200

Revenue.

	G. Crowns.
Jahand, or war-tax, paid by the villagers and townsmen, as not being liable to be called into the field. This is paid in cash and does not vary.	20,000
Revenue, one-tenth of total produce, collected in kind, such as rice, dates, &c.	50 to 60,000
Sea customs only	5 to 6,000
Fisheries	A trifling tax.
Anchorage fees	

There is also a small revenue arising from the Pearl Fishery, but this ought more properly to be considered as appertaining to Bahrein.

There are neither Hindoos nor Christians residing at Kateef at the present time, nor could I procure any person who, in the present unsettled state of affairs, would officiate as a broker. To the accomplishment of this object I had turned my attention, but failed in the completion of the principal wish I had formed regarding Kateef. No doubt the present crisis is extremely unfavourable, as the Turks have been busily employed levying contributions, and the monied men are anxious to screen themselves from notice.

June 28th.—On the morning of 28th Sheikh Mushruf-aal-ul-Arreeur came to me to offer to supply the cattle I required to convey me to Lahissa, under the promise he had made on 22nd instant, and as I could not depend on the influence of the Turk, who was now recalled, and his government of course subject to imbecility, I gladly accepted this offer. The cattle were sent for to his Bedouin camp, at the distance of a few miles from Kateef, on the skirt of the desert, where he had collected them within the last day or two. I received a letter from Mahomed, his uncle, promising every assistance in his power, and as Mushruf proposed to go over to his uncle's camp on the way to Lahissa, I proposed to him to accompany me. The cattle were accordingly brought, and the Sheikh supplied six of his own saddle horses. When we had finished a hasty evening's repast, in which the Sheikh joined, Eusoof Agha was announced; he came from the governor, Khuleel Agha, to request me to defer my departure, as he expected to go off in a few days, and proposed that I should accompany him. Eusoof Agha was at the same time directed to impress me with an idea that I could not depend on the Bedouins. I had received little attention from Khuleel Agha; he had only two deputies, Turks, and about sixty Arabs from the villages, in his pay, and who would now be discharged; he had been himself recalled, as also his deputies, therefore his power ceased. As I did not wish to be troubled with so useless a companion, I selected the Sheikh in preference, and chose to depend on the protection of the Bedouin, who would even in the other case have been called on by the Turk to protect himself as well as me. I sent a reply to the Agha that as Mushruf accompanied me to his uncle's camp, and that as I had paid the Bedouins of this tribe for the hire of their camels, I conceived myself in perfect safety, particularly as I was invited by Sheikh Mahomed to visit him, if possible; and therefore I did not conceive that a further delay would be agreeable to the Pacha, who might justly conceive it to be unnecessary. I therefore committed to this writing, hoping to have the pleasure to meet the Agha at his master's camp and bid him adieu. To Yusoof Agha I made a small present in return for his attention on my landing. He was very desirous to know whether there had been any present sent for the Agha; in reply to which he was told that the Sheikh had supplied the cattle, and probably would expect a present, which, however, would depend on the expedition he used in forwarding my views. He departed apparently well satisfied both with himself and me, as also with the nature of the reply to his master.

Route.—We marched at 6 P.M. from the (W. 2 miles) village of Seehat, and in an hour and half reached Mushruf's (N. 3 miles) Camp of Bedouins, pitched in tents near the wells in the desert, on the skirt of the date plantations, round which we had been passing. Here we encamped à l'Arabe, and lay down in the open plain, the moon shining beautifully bright on the white sand, which resembled the ocean in extent, and in the form or appearance of the surface in many places. We had an abundant supply of water from those wells, which are known by the name of Maā-ul-Bedranee, and are close to the village of Yaroodeeah. The distance from hence to Kateef is about two miles.

June 29th.—On the evening of Tuesday, 29th, we marched at 6 P.M., and had much difficulty to encounter in loading the baggage, although all the loads were remarkably light, the generality being of the size of bullock-loads, as used in India. However the Arabs were determined to save their camels as much as possible, and would not allow any person to ride till the Sheikh interfered. We launched into the desert a motley crew, and marched W. 3 miles; crossed a stream of water; two miles further we came to a small well, where we watered, and then marched seven miles W. by S.; here we halted at three, and lay down in the desert to refresh, as the Arabs were pleased to denominate this kind of bivouac, where there was neither water, forage, nor fire. I used entreaty to induce the Sheikh to proceed, as we had only five miles further to reach our stage, where fresh or sweet water was not to be expected, and our supply of this most necessary article was expending very fast. The Arabs paid no attention to my advice, and made free with every water skin they could lay their hands on; at 5 A.M. of 30th we marched and soon reached the salt wells at Oozoomeeah. Our course was W. by S., five miles. Here we halted, and had but one skin of water for the whole party. I ordered a well to be dug in the hope of procuring better water, but did not succeed. The whole of this march had been over a desert of sand hills and flat sandy plains; the surfaces of the latter were covered with a thick crust of caked salt, through which the cattle sunk very deep at every step, and on these parts there was not a trace of verdure. On the sand hills, which were deep, there were a few tufts of grass and rushes, and some stunted brown bushes, very thickly scattered, and in general a profusion of a shrub which grows in the form of a round bunch or bush; it is very green, full of a saltish and sour liquid, its leaves are thick, of a long oval form, and fully saturated with this liquid; the camels sometimes eat of it, but do not appear to be fond of it or to prefer it. From the ashes of this shrub a strong potash is procured; it is called Ishnan, which appears to be the Arabic name of alkali, or rather the name of the plant from which alkali is procured. The heat during the day was intolerable, and the hot wind of the desert blew in blasts so strong as to render respiration difficult.

An intelligent Arab informed me that there are not any villages in any part of this desert, excepting to the north or north west, where there are seven hamlets containing each from 15 to 150 families in huts, who have a few date trees and a little cultivation. To the west and south-west the whole country is a desert.

June 30th.—Marched at 6 P.M. June 30th, and halted at 9-15 to refresh, as yesterday night. We procured a little bad stinking water; the air was cool, and a few hours' sleep refreshed us after the intolerable heat of the day. Our march had been over sand hills, but we did not pass over another salt plain; tufts of grass and rushes more profusely scattered; some rosemary bushes were the only addition to the plants of yesterday.

July 1st.—July 1st marched to complete our stage at 5-5 A.M. and halted at 7-45 at the well of Maā-ul-Mooliheh. We saw the hill of El-Dam, bearing S. by W. Lahissa, I was told, was immediately behind this hill. To the west of our situation, between this and Oomoorabia there is no water to be procured, and it is two long stages; they said we were not to halt this night, but must proceed on as far as possible, and carry one day's water with us. We watered at the well previous to mounting; the water in it was much decreased by this day's expenditure; it supplies some wandering Arabs, whose abode is in the desert, tending flocks of sheep and goats, of which they have about two hundred. Our visit was not agreeable to them. I doubt whether the Sheikh was as liberal to them as to his own people, who were all supplied with mutton from the flocks of these Bedouins.

July 1st.—Marched at 6-30 P.M. and contrary to expectation we halted after the moon had gone down, but here we could neither procure water nor any other requisite. I was not aware of the determination of the Sheikh to remain till morning, and fell asleep without covering. The Bedouins are certainly the most uncomfortable travellers in the universe; they make no preparation, and have no plan to guide them. The appearance of the desert altered very much in the last march. We quitted those extraordinary sand hills which resembled the billows of the ocean in their form, rising one after the other, and abruptly breaking. I observed that this break was generally towards the south. About 9 o'clock we ascended a rising hill. The depth of sand was not so great, and we passed several hills of this description before our halt at 12-30 P.M.

July 2nd.—Marched at 5 A.M. to complete our stage, and arrived at 8-30 A.M. We saw a very large flock of antelopes—I suppose two hundred,—being the first game I had seen since we set out. Here we halted in the desert for the day, and had the prospect of a long march before we could procure water; halting at night generally caused an unnecessary consumption of our supply.

July 2nd.—Sheikh Mushruf had been very importunate to obtain a present. I had given him to understand that it was my intention to present him with a remembrance or token of my friendship, which I purposed to give him on my arrival at his uncle's camp, which we expected to reach on the morning following. He however prevailed on me to give it this evening, as he said he purposed to go in advance, and he wished to have some testimony of my satisfaction to wear on his arrival. I accordingly prepared what I considered a very handsome present, and sent it to him; he received it and appeared well satisfied. However he shortly returned to my tent, and commenced a conversation respecting the hire of the horses, which I always considered had been lent to me as a compliment, and that the present sent was to satisfy him for all attention shown to the party. He insisted on my paying down ten dollars a head for the horses. As all the people had been paid for their cattle, he was determined to be paid for his, and said that if I did not acquiesce he would march off and leave me where I was. There was no alternative. I was obliged to agree and open my baggage to get the money, as he would not defer till to-morrow his demand. His conduct was that of a barbarian who had got his prey in his power, and determined not to lose the opportunity lest another so favourable should not offer. We had no water, nor could we procure any. I was happy to put an end to the uproar by paying sixty dollars.

A report of thieves having been seen was then spread, but to this I replied that the only thieves in this desert were of his own tribe, and that he could not alarm me on that score; that I should not comply with any requisition he might make for defending me, as he was answerable for my safety. He perceived I was resolute and determined. Myself and three or four of the party being well armed, he thought it too hazardous to play any tricks. My chagrin throughout was a good deal augmented by the recollection that a part of the present which I had sent to this barbarian consisted of a pair of very handsome Cashmere shawls, which the Imam of Muscat had presented to me on my departure, and this circumstance could not fail to present to my mind a contrast in which the Bedouin appeared to still greater disadvantage.

We marched at 7 P.M., having been delayed by these altercations more than an hour and a half. At 11-30 we arrived at the Bedouin camp at Ubwab, composed of three hundred tents; these were of the tribe of Oomoor. Here we halted, and refreshed on some bad water, lay down for the night as usual, and started at 5-20 A.M. of 3rd July. This camp was situated on the border of a salt plain, which was bounded by some broken hillocks. At 8-15 A.M. we arrived at a very large camp of Bedouins of the Beni Khalid tribe, under Sheikh Mahomed and Sheikh Majeed, who were pitched in this plain called Oomerubeah. The former waited on me. He is an old man, very deaf. He was so encumbered with clothes that I am surprized he could bear the load. He did not wear shoes, although the sand was so hot that I could not possibly walk over it. It appeared ridiculous to see a man wearing a costly shawl on his head, thick scarlet cloth robe, and under-robe of gold tissue, and at the same time insensible to the comfort of shoes in a burning desert. Our conversation could not be very interesting, and as the old man was obliged to keep the fast of Ramazan, under a burning sun in this horrid desert, I did not think it would appear polite or hospitable to detain him. Compliments and assurances of friendship having been profusely expended, the old gentleman departed barefoot.

I had now an opportunity to bring Mushruf to an account for his conduct to me in the desert, and had him as completely in my power at the present moment as he thought he had me on the afternoon of the 2nd. I wrote a letter to Sheikh Mahomed detailing the particulars. A large assembly had been fortunately collected at the moment this epistle arrived, which was read aloud to the deaf Sheikh, and consequently heard by the bystanders, many of whom had heard from Mushruf that I had not been liberal to him or to his people. This falsehood soon became too evident. He had neglected to divide a part of the hire of the cattle, and the people became clamorous. The old man appeared sorely vexed at his conduct, and his uncle Majeed came after sunset to offer any recompense for the conduct of the nephew, who had disgraced himself and his tribe. The uncle wished the present and the sixty dollars to be returned, but this I declined, and explained that it was not the value of the one, or the amount of the other, that had induced me to mention the subject; that I felt deeply insulted by the conduct of Mushruf, to whom I had been more than liberal, with a hope of showing his uncles how much I esteemed their friendship, which this breach of confidence and good faith would not cement; that my respect for the Sheikhs was the only inducement to prevent me from referring the subject to the Pacha. To this he replied, I need not refer to the Pacha, as he was determined to produce Mushruf on the morrow and to punish him in a most exemplary manner. Having promised this, I was desirous to change the subject, and allow him time to consider at leisure the consequences to be expected from a repetition of such an insult. After coffee and smoking he took leave, and I retired to bed. Mushruf came attended by two or three decent Arabs. He appeared so truly penitent, and so fully confessed the whole trick, that it was evident the fear of the morrow operated. He threw himself at my feet and implored me to allow him an opportunity of avoiding the disgrace that awaited his past conduct. I thought it prudent to consider his rank, and to seize the opportunity of conciliating his tribe in preference to urging a point which was doubtful, and therefore granted him pardon.

On the morning of the 4th I returned Sheikh Mahomed's and Sheikh Majeed's visits, more particularly with a view to expediting my departure, which was fixed for the evening. The fairest promises and the strongest assurances of friendship were as profusely lavished on this occasion as at the former interview, and both the Sheikhs appeared so well versed in the art of deception, that it was difficult to perceive the motive which induced them to delay providing the cattle. They talked of parties of robbers of the Aieeman tribe having been seen near Lahissa, tried to raise various reports of the dangers to be encountered or expected on the march, all of which was intended as a pretext to raise the hire of the cattle, and to induce me to promise a valuable present. These Sheikhs, as I have seen from the relation in which they stand with their tribes, are the persons to whom a traveller must apply for cattle to convey himself and his baggage, as also for guards to protect it. Should the traveller procure cattle through any other medium, the Sheikh is not answerable for his safety, and would be the first to rob and carry off the booty. I had heard a very favourable report and character of Sheikh Mahomed and Sheikh Majeed, and entered their camp with the expectation of finding them deserving this opinion. Their appearance and address, aided by the assiduity of their assurances, might have led me to place implicit confidence in them, had not the occurrence in the desert fully developed the character of the Bedouin in the person of their nephew, whose first appearance and acquaintance had made the most favourable impression.

Having heard that Sheikh Mahomed purposed to despatch a causid in quest of the Pacha's camp, I requested permission to send a letter by this opportunity to the Pacha's vizeer. The Sheikh promised to forward it.

The 5th July passage in messages, promises, evasion, and professions, and the day closed with a hasty visit from Sheikh Mahomed, who reported all the dangers, impossibilities, and difficulties of proceeding. I closed this interview with insisting on the necessity of my proceeding to Lahissa, as my arrival there would release him from an incumbrance, and free him from all further responsibility. About an hour after his departure Sheikh Majeed arrived, and assured me that we should march the following evening.

I had experienced much inconvenience from not being provided with a horse, and used every exertion to procure one since my arrival in this camp, but owing to the recent disturbances and unsettled state of this country, horses have become very scarce. The few mares that are seen in the Arab camps are kept for breeding. The male foals are seldom considered of sufficient value (in comparison with female) to be reared up. As the owner would be deprived of the use of the dam for several months, the male foals are generally reared on the milk of camels. The few of either offered to me for sale were miserable colts or old mares, and the price demanded was in the proportion of German crowns to Bombay rupees, according to the general usage of that presidency.

July 6th.—I passed this day in misery. The quantity of water I had drank on the march and the bad quality of it has had a very disagreeable effect, which was this day accompanied by fever and thirst which could not be satiated. The hot wind of the desert set in at noon, and continued till the evening, which closed with disappointment. I have only to repeat that the procrastination, duplicity, falsity, deception, and fraudulence of the Bedouin cannot be described by one to an European in language which would present to his mind the real character of these hordes of robbers. To attempt to argue with them on the principles of justice, right, or equity is ridiculous; and to attempt to insist on their adhering to promises or agreements is equally fruitless, unless you possess the means of enforcing compliance. The agreement I had made with Sheikh Mushruf was, that he was to supply a certain number of camels to convey my party to Lahissa, paying four German crowns per head; that we were to arrive in four days, his uncle's camp being only three marches distant from Kateef, and one march distant from Lahissa. I consented to advance three German crowns per head on account of the cattle, and he said he would pay me the compliment of supplying me with his own horses. On my arrival at Sheikh Mahomed's camp I expected from the first interview to have brought Mushruf to a sense of the impropriety of his conduct on the march, and to prevent a recurrence of imposition, but the hoary bearded Bedouin was too well versed in deceit. He said that Mushruf had no authority to hire the people's camels to me further than to this camp; that it rested with himself to agree with me for their hire to Lahissa, for which he demanded two German crowns for each camel. He had promised repeatedly to refund the sixty German crowns. This promise he did not fulfil, and added another imposition to the treachery practised by his nephew.

On the morning of 7th the black tents of the Bedouins began to disappear gradually; their camp presented some bare spots. A march towards Lahissa had been long meditated, and the old Sheikh found himself obliged to comply with the orders of the Turkish officer at Lahissa, although he grumbled very much at the hardship of being obliged to move, having been at the expense of cleaning two or three wells for the convenience of the camp. This might have cost about five dollars for labour. In the evening the cattle arrived for my party, but we did not set off till eight o'clock. We marched by a retrograde route, which course we continued till 3 of 8th, when we halted. I had much trouble in inducing the Bedouin leader of our party to push on to his stage; he frequently attempted to come to a halt in a situation where water was not to be procured, and, according to the old custom, to set off again in the morning. By being very obstinate I carried the point, and we arrived at 3 o'clock at a well which afforded a good supply of water. This spot is called Haffeerah.

We marched from the well at Haffeerah at 7-20 P.M. of 8th, crossed the desert, keeping an E.S.E. course till 6 A.M. of 9th, when we halted at a well of good water called Domeezee. At day-break we passed part of the Bedouin camp at the wells Ein Dar, but the Bedouins would not allow us to halt there. I suppose they did not wish to be troubled with our party, as we would have drawn a large quantity of water, and therefore pushed us off two hours' march, although much fatigued. The men who had been sent as guards behaved very ill these two nights past: they quitted us in the desert, and lay down to sleep. It was useless to speak to them on this or any other subject, and their replies were so impertinent that it was better to avoid altercation with them. It is the usual practice of these Bedouins to appear meek and humble when bargaining with the traveller, who, when he has entered the desert, is completely at the mercy of the lords of the soil, who rule with despotism, and impose at pleasure. If any disagreement takes place, the Bedouins would halt and desert their passengers, leaving them to famish for want of water.

Sheikh Mahomed was encamped to the N.E. at the wells called Salasil.

On the evening of 9th the Bedouin camel-drivers wished to

follow the example of the guards-men of the party, and to join Sheik Mahomed's camp, under pretence of obtaining provisions. As it might have caused the delay of a day, I ordered them to be provided with rice, the only article of which we could spare a portion. Having once more satisfied the impositions of these turbulent barbarians, we marched at 9-15 P.M.; at 11 we passed the village of Hoodia to the left, being the only walled or settled habitation of man that we had met. In its neighbourhood the land is cultivated, and there were several flocks of sheep near the walls. At 7 A.M. of 10th we passed a fine spring of delicious water in a small date plantation, and at 8-15 halted at the village of Jumeah, where there is an abundant supply of water and date gardens. Near this village is an extensive lake which fertilizes the plain, but the salt desert soon checks its operation. I observed some cotton bushes in a garden. Marched at 10-30 P.M. of the 10th. Crossed several high sand hills to gain the direct road, and to enable us to round the head of the lake. We then crossed an extensive salt plain, and keeping a southerly direction reached Labissa at 6 A.M. of 11th. About five miles from Lahissa to the left we passed two large villages, near which there is a lake.

I selected a spot near the fort of Foof, in which the Kashif resided, and pitched my tents in a garden well supplied with water. During this operation a chaws arrived from the Kashif to inform me that a salute was firing in compliment of my arrival. I therefore returned my thanks to the Kashif for this mark of public respect.

On the evening of 12th the Kashif paid me a visit, and on the morning of 13th Khuleel Agha, the governor of Katoef, who, together with his two Turks, had arrived at Ul-Ahsa. Several visits took place between us up to the 17th, and these interviews, which I encouraged, enabled me to form the opinions which I had the honour to lay before the Right Honourable the Governor in Council, grounded on the information which I was then enabled to collect.

Addressed the following letter:—

"To the Right Honourable Sir EVAN NEPEAN, Bart.,
President and Governor in Council, Bombay.

"RIGHT HONOURABLE SIR,

"I do myself the honour to acquaint the Right Honourable the President in council that I arrived at Kateef on 21st June, where I was induced to land in preference to prolonging the voyage by proceeding to Anjeer, which place was represented as very difficult of access, and the communication from thence to Ul-Ahsa as precarious. The governor and two assistants were the only Turks residing at Kateef. In the pay of the governor there were only sixty Arab hirelings from the neighbouring villages, who performed the duty of guarding this place. I was conducted on shore by the second officer, who appeared a man of very inferior rank.

"After a delay of several days it appeared to me that the Turkish Agha did not possess the means of forwarding or protecting me on the route to Ul-Ahsa, and that he himself was dependent on the Bedouin Sheikhs for the protection of the convoys on this road. I therefore determined to place myself under the protection of a Sheikh of the Beni Khalid tribe, and to set out for Ul-Ahsa without further delay. After a tedious and laborious march through the desert, which was rendered more distressing by the conduct of the Bedouins and the impositions of their Sheikhs, I arrived at Ul-Ahsa on the 11th instant.

"On my arrival at Ul-Ahsa I was received with every compliment and mark of attention that the circumscribed means of the Kashif admitted of. He paid me a visit, which I of course returned. The mutual assurances and hope of a permanent friendship being established between the respective governments was the general topic of conversation. The Turkish officers with whom I have had an opportunity of conversing appear to be very ignorant of the Pacha's views; they have been long separated from him, and are completely worn out by the fatigues of three years' arduous service in this sterile and barbarous country; their thoughts and hopes are centered in the expectation of being recalled. The period of their departure appears to have arrived.

" The political state of this country differs materially from the reports which were current in India at the period of my departure.

" The Pacha appears to have found that his troops were too widely extended; that the difficulty of keeping open extended communications in a country which is for the most part a desert would require a large force, to meet the expenses of which the revenues are insufficient, and that little dependence could be placed on the fidelity of the Bedouin tribes. The convoys have been attacked between Ul-Ahsa and Deriah, near Salumiah, which is six days' march from hence. The Bedouin tribe of Saadeh were the perpetrators of this audacious attack.

" The Aieeman* tribe of Bedouins, who traverse the desert to the south of Ul-Ahsa, have lately made an incursion to Anjeer, pillaged the petty fort and the few huts which surrounded it, carrying off the property of a caravan which was about to proceed to Ul-Ahsa. The communication has therefore ceased, and even at this moment the direct route to Kateef is unsafe, several parties having penetrated to the north of this place.

" The Kashif of Ul-Ahsa has received orders to collect the remains of the Turkish troops, amounting to two hundred and fifty, and to rejoin the Pacha's camp at Soodeyur, two marches beyond the site of Deriah, and at which place the Kashif informed me His Excellency purposes to remain for a month. On the departure of the Turkish government the Sheikhs of the Beni Khalid tribe are to assume the government of Ul-Ahsa as tributaries to the Pacha, who claims a portion of the revenues as a remuneration for the expenses of the war, and reinstating this tribe in the dignities and territories of which they had been deprived by the Wahabee.

---

* This tribe furnished the Joassmees of Ras-ul-Khima with a great number of volunteers, who embarked on board their boats for one or two voyages, according to the share of the spoil which was allotted to them.

"His Excellency has razed Deriah, and I am informed that there scarcely remains a vestige of that place, which was so long the terror of Arabia. He appears to have been actuated by another motive than mere vanity. As he did not purpose to garrison this place, it became necessary to render it a ruin,* that it may not at a future period be a rallying point to any tribe of Bedouins, in whom generally little faith can be placed. It is said he purposes to leave a garrison at Anizeh to overawe the tribe of Duwys, which is very powerful, and also as a medium of communication with Ul-Ahsa, that the revenues may be remitted with safety, the continuation of which will of course depend on the stability of the Pacha's power, for although he has been the medium of the present altered situation of the tribe now placed in possession of the territories of Ul-Ahsa, nevertheless the Turks are viewed with much jealousy by these Bedouins, who are anxiously looking for their departure, and consider them at this moment as intruders. The Turks have ruled here with very arbitrary sway, and have been accustomed to enforce their commands over the Bedouins, who are an uncivilized, barbarous race, and probably the most difficult people in the universe to rule or keep in subjection.

"It is evident that the district of Ul-Ahsa, the port of Kateef, and the advantages of the communication by Anjeer, present more favourable prospects than any advantages which could be expected by the accession of Ras-ul-Khima. If the Pacha has found it necessary to abandon these acquisitions, it is not to be expected that he will enter upon any projects for the acquisition of territory which he could not possibly retain, and the acquirement of which would not defray the expenses of the conquest.

"I have laid before the Right Honourable the Governor in Council the only points of information which I have been able to collect since my arrival in Arabia, grounded on which I have

---

* Superstition had a great deal to do with it. As Deriah had been famous for broaching schisms in Islam, and has even produced one or two females who have started new tenets and caused great trouble.

presumed to offer my own opinions of the state of this country, and the views of the Pacha, which appear to be unavoidably directed to the abandonment of all prospects of the acquisition of territory on this coast of the Persian Gulf, and confined to the establishment of his power on the western coast of Arabia, as more closely connected with the establishment in Egypt, and from whence supplies and reinforcements would readily be obtained. The only questions which have been started by the Turkish officers respecting this coast of Arabia have been confined to Muscat, of the political situation of which place they appear very ignorant. The remarks which have fallen from them, however, fully convince me that at some prior period the Pacha had directed his attention to that quarter; the alterations which have taken place in his policy render any comments on this subject unnecessary at the present moment.

"With respect to my further proceedings, I find myself placed in a most perplexed and embarrassed situation. Was I not dubious of incurring the displeasure of the most noble the Marquis of Hastings, I should be inclined to abandon the hope of proceeding on the mission with which I have been entrusted, but as the motives which induced the Governor General to open a communication with the Pacha may not be solely confined to the reduction of Ras-ul-Khima, I conceive it my duty to make every effort in my power to carry His Lordship's orders into effect. The Kashif of Ul-Ahsa purposes to proceed on his route towards the Pacha's camp so soon as he can obtain camels from the Bedouin Sheikhs for the conveyance of the convoy. It would prove a hazardous, and probably an useless attempt for me to set out on such an enterprise, confiding alone in the Bedouins, who may be inclined to avail themselves of the present unsettled state of this country, and plunder the property of the very person who had been entrusted to their charge. I have therefore informed the Kashif that I shall be in readiness to accompany the convoy, and am anxiously awaiting a reply to letters which I addressed from the Bedouin camp to the Pacha's minister. These replies may possibly reach me before the convoy is in readiness to proceed, and from the tenor of them I may be enabled to determine my future proceedings on some more positive evidence than I am at present possessed of.

"I have the honour to be, &c.

"*Ul-Ahsa*, 17th *July* 1819."

The arrival of Sheikh Mahomed and Sheikh Mujeed was announced on the morning of the 14th by a salute fired on the occasion. The following days the Turks were busily employed in their preparations for the journey. The Sheikhs promised to provide cattle, and every person appeared to be in readiness to move. I was soon joined by a horde of Turks, who pitched their fancy tents close by mine, and I found them very disagreeable neighbours, as they took several opportunities to pilfer.

July 18*th*.—I found it necessary to hold a conference with the Kashif on the subject of my further intentions and proceedings, which in the predicament in which I was placed could only be determined by his giving me positive information as to the position of the Pacha's camp, the period of His Excellency's stay in his present situation, and the probable number of days required to enable the Kashif to reach it, provided he moved as he had stated on 22nd. To this the Kashif replied, "that the Pacha's camp was at Soodeynr, which place he would reach in ten or twelve days from the date of his departure from hence, and that he had received a letter from the Pacha intimating his intention of awaiting the Kashif's arrival." The assurances which the Kashif offered were so specious, and he appeared so warm in my interests and the object of my reaching the Pacha's camp, that I determined to accept the voluntary proffer of being provided with a sufficient number of camels from the convoy to enable me to reach the Pacha's camp in company with the Kashif, who assured me "that he would forward all despatches, and that the communication with Kateef should not be closed. That with respect to my return the Pacha could insure that object." To abandon the object of the mission when I probably could in a few days determine, on the most positive evidence, the probability of coöperation and the views and policy of the Pacha, appeared to me to be acting on suppositions which may possibly prove in some points erroneous. Although from the evidence now before me I could form no other opinion on the subject than the conclusions which I had already submitted, I considered it most advisable to adhere to the instructions which I had received, and to make an effort to obtain an interview with the Pacha. I therefore on the 19th addressed a letter to the Kashif informing him that on his assurances and promises I had to come to this conclusion. The verbal reply which he gave to the meerza who was the bearer of this letter (as the Kashif himself has not had the benefit of a liberal education) appeared satisfactory and friendly; he repeatedly promised to fulfil his engagements.

Addressed the following letter:—

"To the Right Honourable Sir EVAN NEPEAN, Bart.,
President and Governor in Council, Bombay.

"RIGHT HONOURABLE SIR,

"I do myself the honour to address you in continuation of my despatch of 17th instant, and to acquaint the Right Honourable the Governor in Council that this evening I held a conference with Mahomed Agha, Cuftun Agasee, and Kashif of Ul-Ahsa. I conceived it necessary to explain to this officer, who fills a very high office, the intricate and difficult situation in which I consider myself placed, and to request of him an explanation on the following points: first as to the probability of my arriving at the Pacha's camp previous to His Excellency's departure, provided that I shall accompany the Kashif's convoy on 22nd instant, the day appointed for his march. To this he replied that he should certainly reach the Pacha's camp at Soodeyur in ten or twelve days from that date; that he would provide a Mihmandar to accompany me; that the Pacha had written to him intimating that His Excellency would not depart from thence previous to the arrival of the Kashif, and that on this point I need not entertain any doubts.

"In reply to my second proposition of keeping open a communication, he has assured me that all despatches shall be conveyed to Kateef. With respect to my return from the Pacha's camp to Kateef, he assures me that he conceives the Pacha possesses the means of insuring that object.

"I have not obtained any information which could enable me to form a more clear opinion on the probable views of the Pacha than the outline which I did myself the honour to lay before your Honourable Board in my letter of 17th instant. The preparations for the departure of the Kashif appear to be in a state of forwardness, and it becomes necessary that I should determine on my future proceedings. Although I do not anticipate the probability of a joint cöoperation of the Pacha's forces, I nevertheless imagine that in abandoning the object of the mission without having obtained an interview with the Pacha, when I find it is not improbable but that a few days may enable me to effect this purpose, and to ascertain on some more certain authority his views and policy, I may probably subject myself to the disapprobation of Government. I have therefore determined to proceed with the Kashif on 22nd instant, and trust that this decision will meet with the approbation of Government.

"I have the honour to be, &c.

"*Ul-Ahsa, 19th July* 1819."

I conceived it necessary to make a suitable present to the Kashif, who I was informed is an officer of rank in the Pacha's army, and therefore on his arrival in camp at noon it was despatched to him. He received it with much satisfaction, and from what I could learn he was perfectly contented and pleased with my deportment towards him.

July 21st.—I thought it advisable to address a letter to the Beni Khalid Sheikhs, and to ascertain from them whether they had determined to afford me their assistance and protection on my return. I had been very anxious for several days to avail myself of an opportunity to confer with them, but the departure of the Kashif, their quarrels with the Aieeman tribe, and several local circumstances, from being more immediately presented to their observation, obliterated the more distant object on which I had before spoken to them, and they deferred this object till my return.

Addressed the following letter :—

"From Captain SADLEIR,

"To SHEIKH MAHOMED and SHEIKH MAJEED,
Aal-ul-Urreeur, Sheikhs of the Bedouin tribe
of Beni Khalid, &c. &c.

"A. C.—Many years have elapsed since your noble family were in the possession of these territories, and in the habits of friendly intercourse with the British authorities. The alterations which have since that period taken place have frequently placed the rulers of this country in the situation of enemies to the British government, particularly during the power of the Wahabee. These territories have been lately rescued from that power, which has now ceased to exist, and have been restored to your illustrious family. It has been my good fortune to arrive at this crisis, and as you have heretofore verbally informed me that your family is desirous of renewing the former friendly intercourse, which may now be effected with so much advantage, at a crisis when it may be desirable that the British government should be acquainted with the alteration which has lately taken place, I shall be happy to be made acquainted with your sentiments. Should they prove to be of the same friendly disposition which you have heretofore expressed, it is probable they may be agreeable to the British government. It is necessary that I should make known to you that at the present moment a ship of war awaits my return to Kateef, which port is of course under your government, and that from the period of my arrival within the boundaries of your territories, on my return from the Pacha's camp, I shall consider myself under your protection till the period of my rejoining the ship in your port of Kateef. This will afford your family an opportunity of evincing your friendly intentions, by exerting your influence in favour of an agent of that government during his stay in your territories.

Seal of
Captain SADLIER.
A true translation.

"*Dated Ul-Ahsa, 21st July* 1819 A.D.
     and 28th Ramzan, 1234 *Hijerah.*"

Sheikh Mahomed, who is very deaf, advanced in years, and unfit to transact business, paid me a hasty visit, and assured me that I might rest satisfied that all my wishes should be accomplished; he could not wait to enter minutely into details; I therefore handed him the letter which I had prepared, and he departed to expedite the march of the Kashif. His answer I received in a few hours, and found it laconic. I closed my packet for despatch by the "Vestal," and entrusted it to Sheikh Khumees, the guide whom I had brought from Bushire. This man's conduct had obliged me to determine on his return. He had been guilty of many deceptions. I therefore gave him an opportunity of returning this evening, under a promise that he would reach Kateef on 24th instant.

The following letter, addressed to Captain Bruce, will point out the precaution necessary to be adopted in selecting guides, and the faith or reliance to be placed in those even of the best characters:—

"*Lahissa, July* 12*th,* 1819.

"MY DEAR BRUCE,

" After the detention at Kateef which I mentioned in my letter, I set off, by the advice of Sheikh Khumees, under the protection of a Bedouin Sheikh (a nephew of Majeed and of Mahomed) whom he introduced to me. As I had declined for several days to proceed in this manner, and did not eventually move till I had received through him the positive assurance of perfect confidence, I entrusted the arrangement of the march, the hiring of the cattle, &c. &c. to Khumees, who reported everything in the most favourable light, and held himself responsible.

"The fifth day Khumees required a present for this Sheikh (Mushruf), to which I objected till we should reach our destination; he persisted, and the Sheikh became impatient. I was obliged to acquiesce, and the present was prepared. Khumees objected to the value which he was pleased to estimate it at (450 piasters), on which I entertained some doubts of his fidelity, and sent the present by my own servant, an Arab. Mushruf accepted it with thanks, but half an hour had not elapsed when he came to my tent and refused to load the baggage, or to send the horses, unless I would pay down sixty dollars for the hire, stating that the present was not of sufficient value to reward him for his trouble.

"Khumees had withdrawn secretly, and sent a private message to Mushruf to which I impute this conduct. I had prohibited him from communicating on this subject with Mushruf on the supposition of his being in his interest more than in mine; the Bedouin acted the barbarian; he refused to allow us to load, and ordered his people to abandon us in this situation, without a drop of water.

"Khumees had taken the precaution to secure a conveyance for himself from the Sheikh, with whom he was prepared to depart.

"On arriving at the Bedouin camp at Oomerrabeeah, I requested Khumees to secure the camels, that we might march in the evening, and gave him this order at 8 A.M. He did not, however, give himself the least trouble about the camels, although he was the person through whom the agreement respecting them was made.

"After a delay of three days I was obliged to send the Meerza, who procured the camels, but not according to the agreement made originally by Khumees; an over-charge of two dollars a head and a further detention of two days were incurred.

"You will perceive it was impossible to stem the tide so long as Khumees remained near me. I have therefore ordered him to proceed to Kateef in charge of letters, and to repair himself to Aboosheer to deliver this letter to you, in which case he may be entitled to the part* of his salary which remains unpaid.

"I remain, &c."

Before I set out from Ul-Ahsa I must offer some description of this district, which is called Ul-Ahsa or Lahissa. The principal or walled town is called Foof; its walls are of mud, and about fifty feet high, surrounded by a deep dry ditch. It has two gates; the houses within the fort are mean; to the east is an open village, interspersed with cultivated grounds and date plantations. Foof and its suburbs do not contain fifteen thousand inhabitants. Of this number probably six hundred may be considered as the effect of its strength.

The fort of Mooburuz is three-quarters of a mile to the north of Foof; its bourjes are lofty, and it is surrounded by a deep dry ditch; it has but one gate; its suburbs or open village is not so extensive as that of Foof, and may contain about ten thousand souls, of which four hundred may be estimated as the effective force. The date plantations extend to the eastward, and are interspersed with open villages and hamlets, which are said to contain fifty thousand souls. These plantations are nourished by an abundant supply of good water from wells and several lakes, but I could not perceive any trace of a river or stream forming a connection between any of those lakes, and to my inquiries on this subject, both Turks and Arabs assured me that no such river exists.

Wheat, barley, and rice are cultivated in the lands adjoining these plantations. The fruits and vegetables of Ul-Ahsa are not good. Those we procured were a few bad apricots, figs very hard and dry, bad water-melons; the onions had the shape of carrots, and not of onions; this is to be attributed to the sandi-

---

* Notwithstanding this constraint or tie, this fellow did not return to Bushire for four months. It was fortunate that I had taken the precaution to send the letters in duplicate by a Causid, who reached the ship, and was paid on delivering them.

ness of the soil and the superabundance of water used in irrigation. The tamarisk tree grows very tall, and is here carefully pruned, as it is of essential use in roofing the houses.

This valley may produce in ordinary seasons a sufficient supply for its inhabitants, but the Bedouins require the whole produce of the date harvest, which, together with the supplies sent into the interior, gives rise to a profitable trade through the medium of the port of Anjeer with Bahrein. Anjeer having been lately plundered by the Aieeman tribe, neither barley nor rice could be purchased at Ul-Ahsa.

In the afternoon the Kashif fulfilled that part of his promise which related to sending the camels, a Mihmundar, and a horse. The camp was disappearing, and we were soon on the move. I had not the pleasure to hear from the Kashif since the receipt of the present, and this evening he mounted and set off without making any inquiries respecting me. The Mihmundar also departed. It appears to me that in a Turkish camp hospitality or attention to strangers does not form any part of their military code. During my stay with the Turks I have as yet received no mark of personal attention from any of that nation.

We marched at 5 P.M. of 21st, and reached the place appointed for rendezvous at 8. At the village of Heweverat, which is walled, surrounded by a large date plantation, and well supplied with water from a hot spring and a large lake, this part of the desert appeared barren and dreary. We passed two camps of Bedouins in their black tents. I compute the distance to be 5 miles N.N.W. of Ul-Ahsa, the range of hills to the west running north and south.

July 22nd.—This day the people were busily employed filling their water-bags. We were to march in the evening by the northern route. During the three first marches the guides did not expect to meet with a single well of water. The Turks would not allow the camels to be removed from the camp to graze lest the Bedouins should drive off the whole. We marched 5-30 P.M., proceeding by a north-westerly course, and halted in the desert at 6-30 A.M. of 23rd. The pickets were very alert. This place is situated on higher ground than Ul-Ahsa. The desert is barren as usual, exhibiting only a few tufts of grass. This spot cannot be much frequented, as there is not a drop of water to be procured.

July 23rd.—Marched at 4-45 P.M. of 23rd and continued our route nearly N.W. till 1-20 of 24th. Here we halted in the neighbourhood of a camp of Bedouins, and lay down till daylight, when we moved about five miles further north and halted at the wells of Oomerrubeeah, the spot on which I had been detained for three days.

July 24th.—P.M. The march was unexpectedly countermanded, and we halted for the night.

July 25th.—A.M. As usual the Turks would not allow the Bedouins to remove their camels from the camp to graze; the camels starving, the Bedouins grumbling, the Turks swearing. Several camels had been carried off by the Bedouins, who had received in advance that portion of the hire which the avarice of the Sheikhs of the tribe allotted to the owners of these animals.

In the evening we marched at 4 o'clock, and not expecting to meet with water, all the water-camels were loaded. Continued till 1-30 a westerly course through a hilly country which was barren, more firm, and not so sandy as the flat desert. Here we halted, and water was discovered in a large well in the plain, which is surrounded with hills. It appeared that this water was supplied by the winter rains which collected in this plat or plain, and this well derived its precarious supply solely from this source. Neither regularity nor precaution was observed in the use of this water, and the well soon became empty. Our night marches were rendered more tardy and unpleasant than on the former march. The convoy consisted of nearly six hundred camels, moving in tens and fifties, each person's baggage forming a separate corps. The moon, which afforded us a cheerful light, was as yet too faint to enable me to mark the route by the compass with any degree of precision. I imagine that the latter part of our route was W.N.W.

One part of the arrangement of our march appeared to me very judicious, and forcibly brought to recollection the justness of the simile which the Arabs so frequently introduce in comparing the desert to the ocean, and in considering the camel as the ship of the desert. An advanced guard, accompanied by the guides, moved on in front under the command of an officer of cavalry, and a large lantern, elevated by a pole affixed to the saddle of a camel, appeared like the top light of a commodore's ship to which the column was expected to pay attention. During the night several pistols were discharged from front to rear to show the position of the different groups, and to prevent their becoming too widely extended.

July 26th.—Replenished our stock of water in the forenoon, which was rather a fortunate circumstance, as the well became dry. We marched at 4 P.M., keeping a W. by S. course, and halted at 8 A.M. of 27th in a high situation. No water procurable; the air rather cooler, and the desert better covered with grass tufts, and bushes. I observed the bable tree * in blossom, and a few wild bare trees, which produce a plum, common all over India.

We saw a few deer, and two or three hares were killed on the march. The only situations in which I have seen deer or antelopes were those where water was not procurable, and as all the wells are too deep for the animal to get at the water without artificial means, I imagine that months elapse without their being able to taste of it. This march was on the beaten road that runs from Ul-Ahsa to Remah.

Marched at 4 P.M. 27th, and continued on the high-road till midnight, when we lost it; the desert becoming sandy, we did not halt till 8 A.M. 28th; route westerly. One Turk died on the march, and several horses. During the stage no water to be procured.

The day was fortunately cloudy and rather cooler. Through the inattention of the camel-drivers, the camel on which the walls

---

* Mimosa.

and poles of my tent were loaded strayed, and the whole for ever lost.

One of the Bedouins picked up a hedgehog on the march, and now brought it to me as a present; the animal was not so large as those I have generally seen in India. My curiosity being gratified, I returned the little creature to the Bedouin, who repeated the Bismillah, and having skinned it, set it on the coals and made an excellent broil. The Bedouins eat all the wild animals they find throughout the desert—the jerboa, the lizard or goana, and even snails, considering all wild animals (with the exception of the hog) as created for the use of man. They have no repugnance to anything provided it has been "hulalled." There are, however, fewer animals in the desert of Arabia than in any wild of the same extent on the face of the globe. Throughout a long march over an open country, where everything is exposed to view, you may probably see a dozen jerboas, three or four hares, which are remarkably small, as many goanas, and probably half a dozen bagra caras or desert partridges, with the breast black, from whence they take their name; there are a few blue pigeons; crows are rarely seen.

July 28th.—4 P.M. Marched three hours west and halted at Remah, where we found a Bedouin encampment of the tribe of Subeeyh, amounting to two thousand families. There are seven very deep wells. I had provided and brought with me four poles, and two wheels to erect a sheers for drawing water. The depth of the wells is thirty-five fathoms, and we used camels to draw up the buckets.

Many of the people had not arrived at the last stage when we set off. Several Persian and Cabul mendicants who had set out with the hope of accompanying this convoy, and ensuring their route to Mecca, died of fatigue and the privation of water. When we moved in the evening there only remained two mushukhs of water from the stock I had brought with me, of which I had been as liberal as prudence admitted. From the situation of this spot, Remah, and the meaning attached to the name—a spear or a place of battles in the centre of the desert—it appears to be a spot of some importance in the desert. If necessary the wells may be easily filled, and there then would remain no possibility of passing by this route; therefore the possession of these wells is a matter of as much consequence in this desert as the retaining a citadel or fortified city would prove on the continent of Europe.

July 29th.—The process of watering occupied the attention of all persons. The Arab encampment removed to some distance to give place to the convoy. Several persons who had been left behind arrived during the day. In the afternoon a thunder-storm, followed by a very heavy fall of rain, upset our camp, and drenched every soul. Night came on before we could repair the damages sustained, which in our situation were of serious consequence; each load was completely water-soaked. The Pacha visited this spot a few months after the capture of Deriah, and punished this tribe for not having obeyed his summons to assist in the reduction of the Wahabee.

I had here an opportunity of witnessing the camel in the performance of a labour to which one would imagine he is ill adapted by nature, and on expressing my surprise at so unusual a sight as that of a camel converted into a draft animal, the Kashif informed me that the Pacha's guns were principally dragged by camels from the Red Sea to Deriah.

The Turks are not much advanced in the sciences of mechanics beyond the Arabs, to whom this laborious duty was generally entrusted; therefore the arrangements of harnessing the animal, or applying his powers to the best advantage, could not be expected from either, although the proof of the ability and fitness of the animal has been ascertained, and may be advantageously improved upon by our Indian armies should their services be required in a similar soil and country.

July 30th.—Marched at 6·30 A.M. We were two hours loading; the camels could scarcely move under the weight of several loads which had been so soaked that they could not be lifted. It was necessary to move from this spot as the Bedouins had been deprived of water for thirty-six hours, and would not submit any longer. Our route was S.S.W. over a hilly country, gravelly surface. In many places the rain-water had lodged, and the desert appeared refreshed by this fall of rain which had done us so much injury. We halted at Sumama at 12, found a small supply of rain-water in a nulla, on the banks of which were several babul trees of a large size. From the appearance of this nulla I should suppose it to be a torrent after each fall of rain in the winter season. The forenoon was cool, and we suffered little inconvenience from the sun. It is worthy of remark that even on the hottest days no occurrence of *coup-de-soleil* had taken place, although the people had been constantly exposed.

To the west of Remah is the province of Nedjd, to the north-east the province of Dehenah, and to the east the province of Sumama. We were now to traverse the province of Nedjd.

July 31st.—Marched at 5-30 A.M.; continued our route along the bank of the nulla. The hills by which it is formed are composed of gravel, covered with large loose stones, and extremely barren. At 10-30 came to the wells of Ul-Begah, in one of which we found some good water. We proceeded till 1 P.M., when we descended from those hills by a very rugged declivity and entered the plain of Aoormuh, where we halted at 2-30; no water to be procured. The first part of our route was S.S.W. along the nulla, we then proceeded S.W., and approached this place by a westerly course. This plain is covered with stones and very barren. In the nulla we found some pools of rain-water, but none in the plain; the nulla runs N.N.E., but is lost in the desert. Aoormuh is a division of the district of Musajidee. We suffered much inconvenience from the scorching heat of the sun during this march, and the evening closed with a thunder-storm accompanied by a heavy fall of rain. The spot on which we had encamped on the plain was very low; a torent of rain-water rushing from the higher ground inundated the camp.

August 1st.—Marched at 6-30 A.M. and descended into a second plain, crossed this plain and a range of red sand hills. We arrived at 12 o'clock at Gah-ul-Bubban, and found a stream of rain-water called Nifooz-ul-Bubban, which induced the Kashif to halt. The sun was oppressively hot. Our route was W.S.W. for the first part, and the latter west. The Kashif despatched several Arabs to gain intelligence of the detachment which he was ordered to remove from Saleemiah, and of which he has not yet obtained any information. This caused us to make a circuit to the southward.

August 2nd.—We marched at 11 A.M. in the direction of Munfooah; halted at 4 P.M. in the mountains. A heavy thunder-storm and fall of rain obliged us to halt here in a miserable plight. The air extremely cold.

August 3rd.—We pursued our route to Munfooah, which bore south, and encamped within a mile of that place, which is surrounded with extensive ruins of walls and boorjes. This points it out to have been once in a more flourishing condition. The site of Deriah is in a deep ravine north-west of Munfooah, about ten miles distant. It is now in ruins, and the inhabitants who were spared, or escaped from the slaughter, have principally sought shelter here. The afternoon closed with a heavy fall of rain and a thunder-storm.

The Kashif sent one-half the detachment in the direction of Saleemiah, to enable the party stationed there to effect a junction. It appears they had been engaged in a quarrel with the Bedouins, and although they were reported to amount to one hundred cavalry, they were not able to evacuate their station and join our party, which was in consequence obliged to make a circuit to the south.

When at Remah the Kashif recommended me to send two Bedouins and one of my own servants one march to the rear, in the hope of recovering the camel and tent which had been lost on 28th, and as he purposed to remain two days at Remah, I consented. The owners of the camel returned to seek their camel, and my man, mounted on a zalool or riding-camel, which I had purchased at Oomerrubeeah, accompanied them. They were unsuccessful in their search, and returned to the wells at Remah about two hours after our departure. My man was seized by the Subeeyh tribe, his arms and camel taken from him, and the murderous sword of the Bedouin was unsheathed to end his existence. He stated to them that he was an Arab of the other coast, and begged them to spare his life. They deferred their decision till the following morning, when he was stripped, and permitted to depart in company with the two Bedouins, who had been treated with kindness by those of the other tribe. These two barbarians obliged this unfortunate man to walk barefoot for four days. They gave him each day a small portion of camel's milk, but would not share one mouthful of the provisions they had obtained at the Bedouin camp; they all arrived here on the forenoon of this day.

The western route from Ul-Ahsa to Deriah *via* Saleemiah is to be accomplished in ten days. The Kashif publicly expressed his intention of proceeding by the usual route, although he had long determined to avoid encountering the Saadeh tribe; he therefore suddenly changed his route to the N.W., and sent an express to order the Saleemiah party to join at Remah, where, not hearing of this detachment, he turned to the south, and thus after a laborious march of fourteen days we arrived here completely worn out with fatigue. During the first part of the march we travelled by night as there was little chance of an attack, in which case our party could not perform the double duty of repelling on the one side, and on the other of guarding their own Bedouin camelmen, who would have been happy to associate with the assailants, or to throw down their loads and desert us, in which case we must eventually have fallen a prey to the one party or the other, as our stock of water, provisions, and baggage must have fallen in their hands. Of the Saleemiah party I was not able to gain any particular intelligence, but from the anxiety expressed by the

Kashif I imagined that party to have been in a very perilous situation.

Awaiting the return of the party from Saleemiah we halted three days, during which I had leisure to visit Munfooah, which contains about two thousand families. In it there are some good houses built of mud and stones, some two stories high, with flat roofs. This place was surrounded with a wall and ditch which the Pacha ordered to be razed. The village of Riad is situated to the north, about a mile distant, and separated by the ruins of walls and houses. Riad is not so well peopled as Munfooah. Each village is surrounded by extensive date plantations, well supplied with water from deep wells. In the winter season the torrents from the barren mountains form a large stream which inundates the valley. The inhabitants were at that moment in a more wretched state than at any prior period since the establishment of the power of the Wahabees. Their walls, the chief security for their property, had been razed, and many of the inhabitants from Deriah found shelter in the date-groves. The year's crop had been consumed by the Turkish force, and there neither remained wheat nor barley to be purchased. In these two villages there was not a horse.

Notwithstanding the wretched condition of these people, they made a show of resistance, and during the first day would not permit any of our party to enter either of the villages. They barricaded their houses, and appeared armed on the flat roofs. Their Sheikh declined to visit the Kashif; for the supplies which they afterwards furnished they extorted at the rate of four German crowns for a sheep, and one piaster was demanded for three eggs; a few bad peaches and figs in the same proportions; watermelons as also musk-melons were very bad; a few brinjals, onions, and some spinage or greens were the only vegetables that I observed. We procured some clover and straw for the cattle.

Camel's flesh of a very bad quality was exposed for sale in an open space near the village, where there was a kind of market held each day since our arrival. Since our departure from Ul-Ahsa such was the scarcity of other meat and provisions that the flesh of the camel was in common use. Whenever, either on the march or in camp, a camel was observed to exhibit symptoms of illness, the Bismilla was repeated, and the knife afforded a speedy release from misery to the unfortunate animal; the flesh was soon separated from the bones, which were not disjointed, and the skeleton remained on the plain to mark our route.

The cotton plant is to be found in the gardens in the neighbourhood of both villages, and at a former period the cultivation of wheat and barley was extensive. Indian corn* is also cultivated.

I was very particular in my inquiries respecting the late heavy falls of rain, which to me was an unexpected occurrence in Arabia at that season of the year. The villagers informed me that such an occurrence had not before taken place within the memory of the oldest Arab in their village, but that during the cold season or winter the weather was usually very cold in this elevated and mountainous district, at which period frequent heavy falls of rain were to be expected. An old Arab of Munfooah, of whom I made some inquiries on this subject, replied to one of my questions by exclaiming, " God is great; I have lived to see three wonders in one day—a Turk and a Feringee at Munfooah, and rain at midsummer!!!"

The only villages which were mentioned to me as being in the neighbourhood of Deriah are Erza, Riad, Munfooah, Doorumbah, Aün, Rumlah. To the south are the villages of Sahmiah, Kharjee, and Khota. The name of Imameh was also mentioned, but it was described as a place of little importance at the present moment, and totally unknown to the Turks. Of the course of a river inserted in many of the modern maps, and made to run close to Ul-Ahsa, I have to remark that there are certainly many torrents formed by the winter rains which shape their courses according to the directions of the valleys between the mountains of this district, but as they are only periodical they ought not to be

---

* Dourah.

magnified into a river. It is probable that the incidental collection of water in those valleys at a certain season, and the great abundance of water near Ul-Ahsa, both in the shape of natural lakes (but totally unconnected) and of wells, reservoirs, and springs, which are to be met with in every direction in its neighbourhood, have given rise to the idea of a river or torrent having at some former period forced its way to the sea. The Arabs at this moment insist that there is a river which passes under ground, the stream of which has never been seen by any human being. They imagine that those springs which gush up are supplied by the superabundance of the waters of this river, and that similar springs in the neighbourhood of Bahrein derive their existence from the same source. This is to be considered rather as a figurative description than as a premeditated falsehood. Kotzebue in his travels in Italy gives an interesting account of the subterraneous streams near Medina.

Our detention at Munfooah was prolonged till 13th of August, when the Saleemiah party reached us, and the following facts transpired. At Kharjeh, near Saleemiah, four Sheikhs of the tribe of Saood resided, one of them named Abdoolah, and another Abdool Uzeez, names which have heretofore appeared very conspicuous in the history of the descendants of Wahab. To these Sheikhs the Pacha had extended mercy and a promise of future protection; he had even presented some with khylats. On His Excellency determining to abandon this side of Arabia, he directed the Chokadar Bashee of Saleemiah to destroy these Sheikhs, but as his party amounted only to fifty men, he did not possess the means of openly effecting his master's order, and resorted to treachery. He invited the Sheikhs to a repast which closed with the assassination of these four men. A few days subsequent to this event a party of one thousand six hundred Bedouins obliged the Turks to take shelter within the walls. From this situation they were released by the appearance of the reinforcement.

To the conduct of the Chokadar is to be attributed the want of confidence in the people of Riad and Munfooah; not a man would venture within the limits of our camp. Those with whom I conversed in the neighbourhood of the village appeared to be implacable enemies to the Turks, and they avowed themselves to be of the Wahabee Faith. Several of their relatives were residing at Ras-ul-Khima, with respect to the fate of which place they expressed and evinced a considerable degree of interest.

August 13*th.*—On the morning of the 13th August we marched at 5; the first part of our route was north; we turned off suddenly to west, and following the course of valleys formed by very barren hills, we reached the site of the ruins of Deriah at 11 A.M. To the west an extensive range of hills extends north-west and south-east, and another range is seen to the north, apparently running to the north-east. These ruins are very extensive, and the remains of walls formed of yellow earth and partially faced with stone, cemented by this earth, mark the site of the principal city, which was closely built on a natural eminence, protected on one side by a deep ravine, and to the west by a range of boorjes connected by a wall.* This western side was denominated Tarefa, and was separated from the eastern town called Sellé, by the principal ravine. This side was also enclosed by boorjes and a wall. The ravine afforded a communication with the other part of the town which was situated to the north

---

* The foundation of the walls was apparently built with large flat stones which are found in abundance in the hills to the north; these were strongly cemented with yellow earth, and of which latter material the upper part of the walls was composed; this earth is very adhesive, and found in abundance all over this part of Arabia; the greater part of the houses are usually built of it. The process of building is very simple. A pit is dug where this earth is expected to be found, and water poured in to mix it into mortar, layers of which are formed of the breadth of the wall by means of a few planks made into the form of a long box; when one layer is completed and dry, another is added, and thus a house is constructed of three or even four stories, the walls of which are one solid mass of this earth, which requires only the labour of the father and his children. Limestone is found near Deriah, but the scarcity of fuel precludes its being brought into use for building, although a sufficiency is procured for white-washing and sometimes for plastering.

and which was not so well protected as the southern. Through this ravine a stream flows throughout the year, and in the winter it is increased to a torrent. In each, however, there are the remains of several good houses now in a state of dilapidation; the walls of the fortification have been completely razed by the Pacha, and the date plantations and gardens destroyed. I did not see one man during my search through these ruins.

The gardens of Deriah produced apricots, figs, grapes, pomegranates; and the dates were of a very fine description; citrons were also mentioned, and many other fruit trees, but I could only discern the mutilated remains of those I have mentioned. Some few tamarisk trees are still to be seen.

Leaving Deriah to the left we soon entered a deep ravine by a very abrupt descent, and continued a W.N.W. route through a sandy run, which appeared to be the bed of a torrent, and halted at 4 P.M. at Oinecah, anciently Deriah; this is an extensive valley of ruins, in which are some inhabitants, and very extensive date plantations and fig trees. This valley has also at some former period been well peopled, but now presents a scene of wretchedness.

It is hardly to be expected that the morals of the Bedouins would be improved by the intrusion of the Turks, and however famed the Arabs may be for the chastity of their females in their secluded state as pastoral Arabs (far removed from an intimacy with the vices of cities), it has unfortunately arisen as one of the concomitant circumstances attending the introduction of a numerous and depraved soldiery, that the morals of these people have become tainted by the introduction of vices hitherto said to be unknown; among them it is very well ascertained that an open or public disregard of chastity has never been noticed by any traveller who may have visited Arabia, and my surprise was called forth by witnessing the misery of several Bedouin girls who had followed the camp from Riaz, and even from Remah. They proceeded generally on foot, dependent on the occasional attention of a Turk, who probably had shared their favours, and in return permitted them to ride on one of his camels, thus forsaking a life of innocence for the most horrid state to which human nature could be debased—that of a common prostitute, following a Turkish camp through the deserts of Arabia.

August 14th.—Marched from Oineeah at 4 in the morning of 14th, continued our route through the valley which opened into a plain, which we crossed, and entering a ravine we ascended another range of hills, from which we descended by a very rugged road into the plain Husseeah, bounded by broken mouldering hills; the road was generally hard and good; the track of the Pacha's guns still visible; and, excepting the descent from the hills of Deriah yesterday, and this rugged road in descending into this plain, little difficulty could have been experienced in conveying the guns. The first part of our route was W. by N.; in crossing the plain we marched west and reached this spot by a W.S.W. course. Here we procured good water from wells. It was 1 P.M. when we arrived at Husseeah.

August 15th.—Marched at 4 in the morning, our route north-west over a table-land, gravelly soil, from which we descended at 6 by a very abrupt, rugged pass, and passed through a valley which led into a widely extended plain. At 10 passed some ruins of walls and boorjes, to which the name of Kussur-ul-Burra is given. Here are a few wells and date trees, but no inhabitants. Our route to these remains of a village was W.N.W., and continuing our march through this widely extended plain we halted at 1 P.M. A boorje, in the corner of a square-walled enclosure, points out this spot, to which the name of Aoorez is given; here we procured water, which was rather bitter, from a few wells. This plain is bounded to the north-east by rugged mouldering hills; the plain extends north-west and south-east: its soil is gravel, very flat, and barren; the latter part of our route was north west.

August 16th.—Marched at 3-30 this morning; our route W.N.W. The desert barren, and the soil gravelly. Arrived at 9-30 A.M. at Surumdah, the walls of which have been razed by the

Pacha. There are some inhabitants residing here, and its date groves are to be seen from a great distance. The grounds in the neighbourhood had been cultivated to a considerable extent, and near it are the ruins of another village called Miriah. Here are several wells, the water of which is not, however, good. In the afternoon it blew a hurricane, and the clouds of sand which floated in the air obscured the sun, although it shone peculiarly bright; the air became oppressively hot.

This was evidently a gust of the Kamsim, and it was fortunate for us that it had set in so late in the day.

August 17th.—Marched at 3-30 this morning; the desert very flat and gravelly; as barren as usual; some large bushes. At 5 passed the village of Quarreen to the left, and at 8 came to some ruins and a few date trees. Our route hitherto had been very direct N.N.W. From these ruins we turned to the west, and passed down a valley to Shakrah, where we halted at 9-30 A.M. The plain over which we had marched breaks abruptly to the west, and from this spot has the appearance of a table-land cut perpendicular. Shakrah is situated very low. The walls of the town appear to have been very strong. It held out eight days against the Pacha's force; he has now destroyed the walls, but the town is not dilapidated. It has a good mosque and market-place. The date plantations which surround the town are very extensive, and plentifully supplied with delicious water from wells, which are very deep. Four Arabs unfortunately fell into one well; only two of them were saved.

We had not as yet pitched our tents when a report reached us that a party of Bedouins of the tribe of Aootibah had driven off all the cattle belonging to the inhabitants of Shakrah. A party from the camp was sent in pursuit, and came up with those marauders, of whom the Turks despatched twenty on the plain, and brought in five prisoners, whose heads were struck off. This tribe has been particularly untractable throughout the campaign, and the Pacha has on all occasions treated them with the utmost severity.

This affair occasioned a general sensation of alarm. Our Bedouins of the Beni Khalid tribe attempted to escape and carry off their camels, alleging that the other tribe would retaliate on them on their return. Two of my party got off during the night, although I had placed all my servants on the watch, and armed them with pistols.

August 18*th*.—Marched at 5. We were delayed two hours in trying to collect our Bedouins, who had secreted themselves; many had escaped with their camels. We crossed the plain from Shakrah to the west, and entered a valley which led into a very extensive desert plain of a gravelly surface, and marched under a burning sun till 1 P.M., when we halted in a barren range of red sand hills, which did not afford either water or forage. During the march we had been tantalized with the appearance of the desert meteor, or vapour called mirage, which seemed to surround us like an ocean. We passed over several thousand colocynths,* which, could we have substituted for them as many real melons, would have afforded our parched throats a most gratifying relief.

The Turks had now passed the limit at which they had promised to release the Beni Khalid Bedouins, and the camels they had hired of them, and which they had stated to the unfortunate Bedouins were to be relieved by an equal number from the tribe of Mootair (Dewys). These Bedouins were now completely in the power of the Turks, who insisted on their accounting for the total number of camels which had set out from Ul-Ahsa. The balance being quickly struck, the Arabs were dismissed without their camels, which were retained to make good the losses sustained by the Turks, in consequence of the desertions which had taken place. Thus the unfortunate men who were really entitled to double pay, having performed a march which required double the number of days stipulated for, were turned adrift in the midst of deserts, surrounded by enemies; they experienced the same treatment which many an unhappy pilgrim had suffered at their hands.

---

* Coloquintida.

August 19*th*.—Marched at 4 this morning, and laboured through the sand hills till 9-30 A.M., when we descended into a plain in which we found an extensive sheet of rain-water collected. Here we halted. Out route was west. There were the remains of a small walled village on the west side of the lake, and some wells which are denominated Aiceoon-ul-Sirr. Throughout this day the sun was oppressively hot. The hot wind blew constantly, even till midnight. The appearance of so extensive a sheet of water, in which we were satisfied from having tasted of it there could be no deception, relieved the mind from the apprehension of suffering. Our imaginations being quieted, thirst was easily appeased.

On the western side of this lake the grounds had been formerly cultivated to a considerable extent.

August 20*th*.—We halted this forenoon to refresh our cattle, and the people marched in the evening about four hours north-west, when we lost our road, and were thrown into such a state of confusion that we were obliged to lie down without knowing where we were. We marched again on the morning of the 21st at 5, and proceeded north-west till 7, when we passed the ruins of some wells and a run of water. This spot had been once cultivated. From thence till 10 we continued the same route and arrived at a walled enclosure which gives shelter to ten or fifteen families. Here also we found the grounds cultivated to a considerable extent, and well supplied with water. At 10 A.M. halted on the side of a lake of rain-water; on its borders we found a supply of grass for our cattle, which had been brought forth by the heavy rains which had recently fallen. This spot is called Aiceooneeat.

August 22*nd*.—Marched at 5 A.M., passed the ruins of a walled village * to the left, and an extensive plain bearing the traces of former cultivation; it is now covered with grass. At some former more happy period this spot may have presented a pleasing

---

* The name of this village is not inserted in my notes; I fear I shall not be able to remedy this neglect.

prospect to the weary traveller. We proceeded N.N.W. till 12-30 P.M., when we halted at a spot called Mooruba, where there are also the marks of former habitations in the plain. In a run of sand we dug and found water. The fall of rain must have been very abundant as the supply of grass was plentiful. The sun had been oppressively hot throughout the day.

August 23rd.—Marched at 5, passed several runs which had been refreshed by the rain, and were covered with grass; these runs conveyed a plentiful supply into the lake called Khubrah, near which are the remains of three bourjes, which gave shelter to the cultivators who annually cultivated this spot. We arrived at Mooznib at 9 A.M. It is an open village, well supplied with wells, the water of which is, however, rather bitter; the date plantations and cultivated grounds in its environs are extensive; our route N. by W.

August 24th.—Marched at 4-30 this morning, passed very barren hills covered with loose stones; our route N.W.; arrived at Anizeh at 12-30 P.M. This place has been rendered a complete ruin; the fort has shared the same fate as all others that fell under the displeasure of the Pacha. Some of the date plantations have been spared. It is situated in a valley, and is abundantly supplied with water from wells. It is considered as the principal town of this district, and from its geographical situation it has been generally the centre of trade. The caravans from Bussorah, Koit, Kateef, Ul-Ahsa, and Deriah, passing through Anizeh annually, have given this place a certain degree of consequence. It is also conveniently situated with respect to Medina and the Red Sea, as also with regard to Jubul Chumber. It has always been the medium of communication between the Persian Gulf and the Red Sea, and might become a post of the first importance from its central position. A garrison placed at Anizeh would overawe the tribe of Anizeh, which occupies the desert to north-east to the limits occupied by the tribe of Mootair, who extend to the east of Shakrah in the direction of Koit; from thence, towards the Persian Gulf, the Beni Khalid tribes extend to the south as far as Ul-Ahsa;

to the south of which district the principal is the refractory tribe of Aieeman, which, however, is not sufficiently powerful to oppose the Beni Khalid tribe; to the south-west of Deriah is the Ooteiba tribe,* which has been nearly exterminated, and to the west of Anizeh the tribes of Hurab and Misroo, which occupy that part of the district of Al Hejaj between Rus and Medina. Thus the town of Anizeh appears to be the centre of Arabia in a geographical, political, and commercial view. I met several merchants from Koveit and Zobeir, who were of the Ootoobee tribe, both at Shakrah and Anizeh, and we found a supply of Indian rice and other articles in the bazars.

August 25th.—We marched at 6 A.M., and entering a range of red sand hills, we laboured through them till 12-30. In valleys formed by these hills we saw the remains of wells and the traces of former cultivation, which proves that the peasants ventured to detach themselves from the city. Our route was westerly. Here we found a supply of rain-water.

August 26th.—Marched at 5 this morning, and pursuing a westerly route we arrived at Rus at 1 P.M. Daily reports reached us that the Pacha awaited our arrival at this place, and I approached Rus with the anticipation of my labours being brought to a close in the course of a day or two, when I might expect to set out for Bussorah on my return to India. I had sent messengers to apprise the Minister of my arrival. In vain did they search and inquire for the tent of the Chaia or of the Pacha. I awaited their return as long as I could bear the scorching rays of the sun, which obliged me to push forward in the hope of procuring shelter or shade and a little water to satiate thirst, which had become oppressive. I entered a confused medley of tents, some belonging to Turks, some to Bedouins of Arabia, and others to Bedouins of Barbary, and a few to the Arnaoots. I therefore pitched mine, and added to this heterogeneous assembly my suite of Persians, Indians, Portuguese, and Armenians. My

---

* The Ooteiba tribe and Ootoobee tribe are not one and the same tribe, as will appear by the text.

disappointment was rendered the more painful when I waited on the Effendi, who had been deputed to officiate after the departure of the Pacha, who had set off post for Medina on the day we arrived at Anizeh. I found Mahomed Effendi, entitled the Dewan Effendissi or Chief Secretary of His Excellency's court, to be as little acquainted with the geography of the very country in which his master had been employed in a three years' war, as a child who had never departed from the walls of the city of Cairo. I found it necessary to request an escort, agreeable to the assurance of the Kashif, that I might effect my return to Bussorah. To this the Effendi replied by assuring me that without orders he could not comply with my wish to return to Bussorah, which would be a most hazardous undertaking, to the responsibility of which measure he was not inclined to subject himself. The Effendi informed me that the route from Medina to Bussorah would be much more easily effected, and would require a shorter period. As I would not agree in this opinion, he next proposed a journey to Bagdad *via* Syria, which could, as he stated, be accomplished in twenty days. I urged him to furnish the escort, and even stated my intention to procure guards from the tribes, but found the ignorant Turk firm in his determination. I was obliged to desist, and to look forward to the Red Sea in place of the Persian Gulf to obtain a release.

This Minister promised, however, to enjoin the Sheikh of the Anizeh tribe to forward my letters to Bussorah, for which purpose I had found it impossible to procure a special causid; such is the state of Arabia.

Addressed the following letter:—
" To the Right Honourable Sir EVAN NEPEAN, Bart.,
            Governor and President in Council, Bombay.
" RIGHT HONOURABLE SIR,

" I have the honour to acquaint the Right Honourable the Governor in Council that I departed from Ul-Ahsa on 21st July under the protection of the Turkish troops which lately occupied that district, the direct route from whence by Saleemiah to the site of Deriah is stated to be ten days' march, and by this road the Kashif publicly expressed his intention of proceeding. He, however, conceived it politic to change his route, and on the second day's march directed his course to the north-west to the wells of Remah, at which point he expected to be joined by the garrison of Saleemiah. The Kashif was induced to change the direction of his march from the probabilities of his party being attacked by the Aieeman tribe, or by the tribe of Saadeh, which had cut up the last convoy proceeding by that route. On arriving at Remah we learned that the Pacha had moved from his late camp near the ruins of Deriah, but I could not obtain any precise information as to the direction he had pursued. The garrison of Saleemiah was not of sufficient force to move from the walls of that petty fort, and the Kashif was under the necessity of proceeding south to Munfooah, where he halted on 3rd of August. He sent forward half his force be enable the Saleemiah party to evacuate their post.

"Our detention at Munfooah was prolonged till the 13th of August, when the Saleemiah party reached us, and the following facts transpired. At Kharjeh, near Saleemiah, four Sheikhs, descendants of Saood, resided, one of them named Abdoollah and and another Abdool Azeez, names which have heretofore appeared conspicuous in the history of the descendants of Wahab. To these Sheikhs the Pacha had extended mercy and a promise of future protection; he had even presented them with kheelats. On His Excellency's determining to abandon this part of Arabia, he directed the Chokadar Bashee of Saleemiah to destroy those Sheikhs, but as his party amounted only to fifty men, he did not possess the means of openly effecting his master's orders, and resorted to treachery: he invited the Sheiks to a repast, which closed with the assassination of these four men. A few days subsequent to this event a party of one thousand six hundred Bedouins of the Aieeman tribe obliged the Turks to take shelter within the walls. From this situation they were released by the appearance of the reinforcement.

"This transaction has been attended with very unpleasant consequences as far as relates to my return to Kateef, which point I had endeavoured to secure by obtaining from the Beni Khalid Sheikhs a written promise to that effect, which is now rendered useless, as the whole country is in arms. Another breach of faith on the part of the Kashif has placed it out of my power to effect my return. On our departure from Ul-Ahsa he solemnly promised that the Bedouins of that tribe should be allowed to return with their camels, which were to be relieved by an equal number furnished by the tribe of Dewys. The Kashif, far from fulfilling his engagements, has seized the camels of the very tribe which afforded him the means of quitting Ul-Ahsa, and I can no longer look to those men for protection on my return, or depend on them for the conveyance of any communication with Kateef, at which port the Honourable Company's Cruizer has been stationed for the conveyance of my letters.

"On the march from Munfooah I was enabled to visit and ascertain the present state of Deriah, which is situated ten miles N.W. at the head of a deep ravine formed by very barren mountains. The walls which surrounded the town, the forts, and several houses have been razed. The Pacha was determined to render this spot a wilderness, and previous to his departure caused the date plantations and gardens to be destroyed. At the present moment there is not a single family inhabiting its ruins; those who had the good fortune to escape from the ravages of war have taken shelter principally in the town of Munfooah, which contains about two thousand families. In this town there are some good houses, on the flat roofs of which the Arabs appeared armed, and prepared to oppose our entry. The Pacha had destroyed the walls and boorjes which served as a security for the property of the inhabitants against any attacks of the Bedouins. The village of Riad, separated from the former by extensive ruins, has been also deprived of its defences; but the date plantations in the neighbourhood of both have been spared. The scanty harvest of the present year has been consumed by the Turks; and in this district there is not a horse to be seen. The Sheikhs of these villages, although placed in authority by the Pacha, refused to obey the summons of the Kashif to pay him the respect of visiting him in his camp.

"His Excellency's army was eight months occupied in the siege of Deriah, since which period the troops have been busily employed in retaliating on the Bedouin tribes. The most trifling acts of misconduct have served as a pretext for depriving them of their flocks. The defences of every village in Nedjd have been destroyed; and if the walls of Ul-Ahsa have been spared as being too remotely situated, the Kashif did not show the same respect for the private purses of the inhabitants, from whom he extorted twelve lakhs of piasters previous to his departure from that district. This policy was not resorted to by the Pacha till he had formed the intention of abandoning this side of Arabia, when he determined on these measures, by which he enriched himself and his army, and by laying waste the country to a degree that it has never before presented, he expects to reap the advantage of the tranquillity of the possession on the western side of Arabia.

"I lament that I have to acquaint your Honourable Board that I have been dragged a reluctant witness of the devastations of the Pacha's army as far as the ruins of Rus, from whence His Excellency set off express for Medina but two days previous to my arrival, leaving an Effendi here to officiate. I have waited on this officer to require the fulfilment of the promises under which I consented to depart from Ul-Ahsa, but which has been rendered impracticable by the conduct of the Turks themselves, as I have already brought to the notice of your Honourable Board. It therefore remained for me to propose the only expedient that now offered, namely, a safe guard to protect me to Bussorah, which is only twelve marches from Anizeh, and within nine marches I should have met with the Montefick Bedouins, with their chief. Captain Taylor kindly arranged a safe return for me to Bussorah. Had this proposal appeared to me as impossible, I should not have urged the request, the denial of which will oblige me to proceed to any port in the Red Sea from whence I may possibly find a conveyance to India, without there remaining for me a possibility of effecting the object of the mission on which I have been deputed.

"I have the honour to be, &c.

"*Rus, 26th August* 1819."

August 27th.—A few of the Bedouins who were the rightful owners of the camels which had conveyed us from Ul-Ahsa to Rus being now on their return, I engaged some of them to convey my leters to Kateef and Ul-Ahsa.

August 28.—Marched at 5-30 A.M. over a gravelly barren plain, skirted to the west by a range of rocky hills; passed some hamlets which had been inhabited at the Pacha's advance, but now deserted; halted at 10-45 at the wells of Mutta, which are still marked by a walled enclosure, giving shelter to a few families who cultivate the grounds close to the wells. Our route S.S.W.

August 29th.—Marched at 5. The morning air very cold; crossed a second gravelly plain very barren; halted at 10-45 A.M. at the wells called Uddas. We had here a view of barren mouldering hills detached from each other and scattered in every direction over this widely extended plain. Our route was W. by S.

August 30th.—Marched at 4-30 A.M. Continued our route over the same plain till 12, when we entered a valley which led us into the range of hills which run north and south. We ascended gradually, our hungry camels feeding as they passed on the coarse grass which abounded in this valley. We descended into a hollow on the other side this range, where we found some wells. This spot is called Jirzaweah. It was 3-30 P.M. when we halted. These rocky hills are very bare, but appear to be a principal range, although of no considerable elevation. Our route was west.

August 31st.—We were disturbed at 1 o'clock this morning; loaded our cattle and unloaded them; the Turks always in confusion, and without arrangement; they never plan any movement. We lay down till 4-30; marched over a very extensive plain of fine gravel strewed with the usual bushes, and bounded by detached rocky hills to the south; at 10 entered a range of red sand hills; in the hollows were the marks of pools of rain-water. At 1-30 emerged from those hills, and halted in a plain which had been lately inundated. This spot is called Wadee-ul-Meeah. Our route was west. In the winter this plain remains constantly under water. The regular stage is to the wells of Bajeer, which bear W.S.W.

September 1st.—We marched this morning at 5, crossed a very extensive gravelly plain; proceeding west we entered a sandy run through which the winter torrents reach these plains. We expected to have found the water brackish, and had loaded every camel with water. On halting at 3-30 P.M. we found an abundance of fresh water by digging wells. This is to be ascribed to the unusual fall of rain at this season. This spot is called Mushash Batin-ul-Aoormeh.

September 2nd.—We marched at 4-30 A.M. and crossed the western part of this plain, which is sandy, but tolerably firm and level. Jubul Maweeah bore W. by N.; it is discernable at a great distance, the plain being a flat. We moved round the north end, and halted to the west of the mountain at 1 P.M. This place is rendered memorable, as here Abdoolah first opposed the advance of Ibrahim, having a force of ten thousand men on dromedaries, which was soon routed by a few hundred horse under the command of Aoozoon Alee. The valley is still strewed with the bleached skeletons of Wahabees.

September 3rd.—Marched at 4-30 this morning over a broken hilly country; proceeding west we entered a valley from which a torrent of winter rain passes to south-east; here we found wells, at 11-30 watered. This being completed we continued a westerly route through a plain interspersed with rocky hills, but unattached to each other; these hills were of bare rock. At 12 at night we came to the principal range, which appears to run north-west and south-east, and passed through the Derah of Humeej; here we expected to find water, but being disappointed, the advance of our party proceeded, and we became separated. I proceeded with the advance, and we continued to move on slowly till 10 A.M. of 4th, when we reached Heneekah; here we found a Turkish post under the command of a man denominated Ujum Oglan (the man of Persia). He proved to be a hospitable soldier and a native of Tebreeze: he treated me with much attention, produced the best of everything he had in store, spread his carpet, took care of my horse, and having refreshed me with bread, coffee, and pillow, he prepared a place for me to sleep. At 3 P.M. the rear party and the baggage arrived, and continued to creep into camp till 7 A.M. of 5th.

Heneekah has been a station for a detachment to cover Medina and check the Bedouins of Nedjd, which is here separated from the Hejaj. The supply of water is plentiful and forage abundant. Here is a small mud enclosure with four bourjes, in which are four small guns. The detachment was reinforced from our party to two hundred men. The nulla which waters the plain is confined by a wall of stone rudely constructed. It, however, answers the double purpose of preventing the winter torrents from suddenly overflowing the flats (which are generally cultivated every year, and afford the chief supply to Medina), and also retains the water for several months, which with the additions of wells, enables the cultivators to procure a plentiful crop.

September 5th.—We marched this evening and proceeded at first south-west across the bed of the nulla and a plain covered with loose stones; we then entered a gravelly, barren plain, bounded by rocky hills. The runs descending from these fertilize a few spots in the plain. These were generally sandy, strewed with bushes and grass tufts and some bauble bushes. We entered a Derah between the hills, and descended into a deep rocky ravine in which is a plentiful supply of water; here are also the remains of walls to support the banks. The hills surrounding this ravine are high, rocky, and barren; in its bed are several large bauble trees of the brab species: these differ in having several branches; the leaf resembles the brab, and the fruit appears to be of that species; the tree is called Down,* and the fruit, which partakes of the flavour of ginger-bread, is called Bhash. It was midnight when we reached this spot; we performed a good march; the air was cool, and the moon shone bright; my compass was unfortunately rendered useless by the constant jolting.

September 6th.—Marched from the ravine at 3 P.M., and proceeding over a rocky mountain road, we entered a valley which is sandy, and affords some forage; this terminates in the plain reaching to Medina. This plain to a considerable extent is covered with loose stones, is extremely barren, and presents a most sterile aspect. We halted at 3 in the morning of the 7th, at a spot which was supposed by our guides to be the regular halt. However at daylight we found we had fallen short of the mark, and reloaded, as I supposed, to proceed to Medina. An order from the Pacha directed the whole should halt till noon, when the detachment was to proceed to Medina.

Christians not being permitted to enter the city of Medina, His Excellency directed his Peshkur Aghasee to conduct me to Bir Alee, which is to the west of Medina. There His Excellency's harem and family were encamped. We proceeded by a circuitous route, avoiding the city; the Peshkur Aghasee offered to conduct me by the direct route near the city. He, however, remarked that I might feel displeased should any zealots or devotees meet us, as they would not fail to offer remarks which it would be difficult to silence so near the holy city, where the Turks are obliged to deport themselves with deference towards the priests of the shrine and the Moolahs. This was the first instance since my arrival among the Turkish soldiery that I had heard the subject of religion introduced.

The dress of an European passed unnoticed, and the soldiery had throughout this long and fatiguing march invariably conducted themselves in a very respectful manner towards me. I felt a strong inclination to visit the city or to obtain a goo dview, but

---

* Palma Thebaica.

prudence forbade me to expose myself to insult. I had now entered the land of Mahomedan superstition and fanaticism. I therefore requested the Agha, as he had been deputed as my guide, to lead the way and I should follow him. We proceeded by a road to the north of the city, and rounding a lofty rocky mountain,* passed the ruins of the village of Birkas, which once contained two hundred houses. It at present gives shelter to about sixty inhabitants. In the plain there is an abundance of pasture, and a stream of good water and several wells. We then crossed a stream of bitter water, which passes through the city, and proceeded to Bir Alee, through a valley in which is the bed of an extensive torrent which is supplied in the winter from the mountains. I arrived at 9 P.M. very much fatigued. His Excellency's Hukeem Bashee, Doctor Antonio Scott, an Italian gentleman who has the medical charge of the Pacha's family, had prepared a Turkish supper, which at this late hour, and in the absence of all other immediate refreshment, proved acceptable.

Just as we had entered the valley leading to this spot my horse, unable to bear my weight any longer, fell under me; the animal was so fatigued that he was totally unequal to the exertion of reaching the tents, the lights in which were then visible. I was obliged to strip off the saddle and mount a camel which was nearly as much jaded as the horse. We had been thirty hours on the march, during which we had watered only once.

September 8th.—The Pacha arrived at 9 o'clock this evening, and alighted at the tent of the Hukeem Bashee, His Excellency not having any other personal accommodation than the tents of his harem prepared at Bir Alee. His retinue was not numerous, but in general richly clothed and armed. He deputed the doctor to request that I would pay him a visit without entering on ceremony or business, which would be deferred till a more suitable hour on the morrow. I therefore complied and was received courteously. Coffee and pipes were then introduced. The cup

---

* Probably the mountain of Ohod, mentioned in the third chapter of the Koran, rendered memorable by the defeat of Mahomed's army.

presented to His Excellency was placed in a zerfinjan set with diamonds; those presented to other folks were held in undercups intended to pass for silver.

His Excellency entered into a long apology on the subject of the march and inconveniences which I must have suffered, stating that my return from Rus or Anizeh would not have met with his approbation as the route was not safe; that very urgent business had obliged him to set off from Rus, but that these delays and disappointments were unavoidable.

I replied to His Excellency that I had been particularly desirous to reach his camp at Deriah, as it would have afforded me an opportunity to offer to His Excellency the congratulations of the Most Noble the Governor General on the very spot where the arms of the Ottoman Empire, under the command and guidance of His Excellency, had obtained so signal a victory. His Excellency appeared highly gratified when informed that the news of his victory had reached so far as Calcutta, and that the result had been so fully appreciated. He said he was very desirous to be known personally to the English authorities in India, with whom his father had always been on the most friendly terms; that his father had at all times coincided in every request of the British, and was particularly desirous on all occasions to evince his inclinations to establish a permanent friendship with the English in preference to all other European nations. The Pacha entered into a long inquiry about India, the extent and riches of the country, the number of troops, and cities, ships of war, &c., and appeared very desirous to obtain a general view of the whole during the one interview.

This visit was protracted till 12 o'clock; coffee had been so often introduced and pipes so frequently refreshed, that I feared it would not have been brought to a close ere morning. The Pacha during the visit appeared to wish to impress on my mind the idea of his being a very affable soldier. He presented me with a pinch of snuff from a very beautiful diamond snuff-box and on retiring said that as his stay at Bir Alee could only be prolonged till the following afternoon, he would be happy to confer with me at my tent in the morning; His Excellency then retired to his harem.

On the morning of 9th His Excellency walked over from his harem, bearing his eldest son Osman Bey in his arms; his daughter Fatima was borne in the arms of an officer of his retinue. I met His Excellency at the entrance of the tent, and conducted him to a chair, on the right and left of which two chairs were placed, the one for the accommodation of the Hukeem Bashee, who is entitled to sit in the presence of the Pacha. His Excellency renewed the conversations of the foregoing evening, and I availed myself of an early opportunity to present to His Excellency the despatches of the Most Noble the Governor General and the Right Honourable the Governor in Council of Bombay, both of which His Excellency appeared to peruse. His Excellency, addressing himself to me, remarked that heretofore he had been only known to that Government through the medium of the friendly correspondence which had existed between his father and the British authorities in India. I replied that the present communication was the foundation of a personal and more permanent friendship which I hoped would be continued without any interruption. I then presented to His Excellency the sword which had been entrusted to my charge for that purpose. His Excellency appeared highly gratified. He examined the workmanship of the scabbard with attention, and on drawing the blade he declared it to be one of the most elegant swords he had seen, availing himself of this opportunity to compliment the Governor General on the taste displayed in the selection of this favour.

After a short complimentary conversation His Excellency directed the attendants to withdraw, and a second time perused the letters which I had the honour to present. He entered into a long detail of the transactions at Deriah, the destruction of which city had originated in orders from Constantinople. He expressed his regret that he had not been acquainted with the plans or views of the Governor General at an earlier period. His

Excellency inquired very particularly whether any communication had taken place between the higher authorities on this subject. I could only reply that I had not been informed whether any such communications had taken place or not. The Pacha stated that he did not consider himself at liberty to frame a reply on a subject of such importance without referring to his father, whose orders would enable him to offer a suitable reply to the despatches which had been presented.

As I felt an anxiety to avoid any further detention, I expressed to His Excellency my desire to return to Bombay with all possible expedition, and as the port of Jeddah promised the most probable chance of procuring a vessel, I requested His Excellency to reconsider the subject of the despatches, and if possible to avoid the delay which must ensue from referring the subject to His Highness the Viceroy of Egypt, to whom, although the reference might prove very flattering, nevertheless, excepting that some very peculiar advantage was expected to be derived from the reference, I entreated His Excellency not to prolong the period of my detention, but to form his reply and permit me to accompany him on the route towards Mecca, and thence to Jeddah, from whence I could forward copies of the communications to Mr. Salt, who would lay them before the Pacha, and explain the motives which induced me to request a reply without awaiting His Highness's counsel.

His Excellency declined framing any reply, stating that he did not conceive that he possessed that privilege; that he would feel happy in forwarding my views at Jeddah, where I might await his return from the Hej, by which period the reply from Cairo would arrive, and the whole affair would then be brought to a happy conclusion. His Excellency requested me to address a letter to Mr. Salt detailing the nature of the communications I was authorized to make, and which I had explained verbally to himself.

The Pacha then informed me that the policy of this expedition had been directed by his father under the orders of the Porte;

that he himself had been entirely ignorant of the extent or ultimate views which had induced the Ottoman court to set on foot the expedition. His orders had limited his operations to Deriah, after the fall of which place he awaited the further instructions of his father. During this delay he had pushed a post as far as Ul-Ahsa and Kateef to procure supplies, his army being in the greatest distress, and that at that period a friendly intercourse with the British would have been of the first importance. With their assistance the removal of a part of his force might have been easily arranged; the principal difficulty which opposed these plans was the removal of artillery, which by the presence of a naval equipment would have been obviated.

His Excellency informed me that the Imam of Muscat had written a letter to His Excellency offering to employ his vessels against the Joassmees whenever the Pacha would point out a favourable opportunity; that on the fall of Deriah, and the advance of the Turks to Ul-Ahsa, His Excellency had written two letters to the Imam, but as no measures had been adopted by the Imam for furthering these plans, the Pacha had abandoned the intention.

I conceived it my duty to acquaint His Excellency that the amicable and cordial intercourse and correspondence which had hitherto existed between the Imam of Muscat and the British Government, induced the Government of Bombay to place the fullest reliance in the exertions of the Imam to promote the views of Government in the intended expedition, and that the Imam had pledged himself to me to that effect. This consultation led to the following conclusion.

From the result of a reference to His Highness the Viceroy of Egypt little more could be expected than a complimentary reply, expressive of his consideration of the favour conferred on his son, and the light in which the result of the war against the Wahabee power has been viewed by the British authorities in India, which, in the event of any future operations in which the interests of the two powers may be combined, would probably lead to a combination of the resources of the two Governments, and more fully prove to His Highness the intentions of the British Government in India to cement the unvarying friendship and good-will which His Highness has hitherto manifested.

His Excellency Ibrahim Pacha appears highly gratified by the complimentary congratulations of the British Government, and the appropriate favour which has been conferred by the Most Noble the Governor General. The present communication will no doubt influence His Excellency in any future intercourse which may occur between His Excellency and any of the constituted authorities of the British Government, and may possibly be productive of mutual satisfaction.

The object of the mission relative to a joint cöoperation against Ras-ul-Khima has proved impracticable from circumstances which could not have been foreseen. The advanced season of the year now precludes a remedy being applied, or measures being adopted which would in any wise aid the undertaking.

In consideration of the foregoing conclusions I am induced to gratify His Excellency by awaiting the result of the reference to His Highness, and to address a letter to Mr. Salt explaining the communications which have taken place, and requesting him to use his influence to expedite my departure for India.

The deliberations having been concluded, His Excellency expressed a wish that breakfast should be prepared, in which he was shortly gratified. The etiquette of a Turkish breakfast requires that each dish should be produced in rotation, and that each guest should eat out of the one dish at the same period, using only a wooden spoon. Breakfast being announced, His Excellency took his seat at the head of the table, and did not appear embarrassed. He used his spoon, fork, and knife very dexterously, and made a hearty breakfast. The only part of an English breakfast which he did not appear to relish was tea, and this he could not use. A bowl of sherbet was therefore introduced as a substitute, after which coffee and pipes closed the scene, and His Excellency remained till 11 conversing on different subjects. The Persian attendants attracted his attention, and this led to a long conversation on the subject of the late connection between the British Government and the King of Kings, of whom His Excellency did not appear to entertain a favourable opinion. At 11 His Excellency returned to his harem to repose till the afternoon, when he set off for Medina.

September 10*th*.—His Excellency having communicated to me his intention of despatching a courier to Cairo, I availed myself of this opportunity to address the following letter :—

" To HENRY SALT, Esq., F.R.S.,

Her Majesty's Consul General, &c., Egypt.

" SIR,—I have the honour to transmit a letter from the Chief Secretary of the Government of Bombay to your address, and to annex copies of the despatches addressed by the Most Noble the Governor General and the Right Honourable the Governor in Council of the Presidency of Bombay to His Excellency Ibrahim Pacha, commanding the Turkish army in Arabia. From the perusal of these despatches you will be informed of the ground on which the British authorities were induced to address His Excellency, and of the object of the mission on which I have been deputed.

" I arrived at Kateef on 16th June in one of the H. C. C., and from thence reached Ul-Ahsa after a painful journey. I had the mortification to find that the political views of the Pacha presented a prospect the very opposite of the expectations which had been formed from the reports which had lately reached the British authorities in India, and that His Excellency's departure from Arabia was not far distant. Considering the grounds on which the Most Noble the Governor General had addressed himself direct to Ibrahim Pacha, and that it would probably afford His Highness Mahomed Ali Pacha much satisfaction to learn that the result of the late enterprise had been so fully appreciated, I conceived it my duty to undertake a journey to His Excellency's camp which I was assured would not exceed ten or twelve days.

" Many unexpected and unlucky incidents prolonged our march, and His Excellency's early departure on his route for Medina obliged me to accompany the Turkish detachment to Rus, from whence His Excellency had set off express for Medina the day previous to my arrival. I endeavoured to effect my return to Bussorah, but the state of Arabia at the present moment rendered such a journey impracticable without an escort, and this the Turkish officers were not at liberty to grant without an order from His Excellency. There remained for me no other alternative than that of proceeding to Medina, where I arrived on the 7th instant, having performed a most laborious journey during the most unfavourable season of the year through a desert country, which is now rendered a waste by the destruction and devastations of war.

"His Excellency deputed an officer, Mahomed Agha, Peshkur Aghasee, to conduct me to Bir Alee, three miles distant from the city, at which place His Excellency's family is encamped, and where my residence has been honoured by the presence of His Excellency. Dire necessity had certainly driven me to Medina, and although it was very evident that one object of the mission on which I have been deputed could not be effected, I considered it my duty to present to His Excellency the despatches which had been confided to my charge, as also the sword intended for His Excellency, who received it with the highest degree of satisfaction. These pledges of the sincerity which actuates the British authorities in India in their desires to cement the unvarying friendship and good-will towards the British Government, which His Highness the Viceroy of Egypt has evinced his inclinations to foster and strengthen, and which feelings I trust will actuate His Excellency Ibrahim Pacha in any future intercourse with the constituted authorities of the British Government, which no doubt would be productive of much mutual satisfaction. These motives and expectations will, I trust, be considered perfectly consonant with the address of the Noble Marquis to His Excellency Ibrahim Pacha.

"His Excellency expressed the deepest regret at the altered state of affairs, and the delay which had occurred to frustrate the inclinations which actuate him in his desires to meet the wishes of the Most Noble the Governor General, in whose views he would have been most happy to have coincided at an earlier period had he been acquainted with the intention of the British authorities in India, and expressed his desire to communicate the subject to His Highness the Viceroy of Egypt, as he considered it a matter of such importance as to require a reference, on the supposition that possibly some communication may have taken place between the Governor General and the Viceroy of Egypt, with which His Excellency is unacquainted. I therefore availed myself of the intention of His Excellency to despatch a courier to Cairo, and to lay before you the general outline of the communications which have taken place.

" His Excellency Ibrahim Pacha was very desirous to ascertain the extent of the assurances which I was instructed to convey in the event of a cöoperation of the two forces, and the certain result of such a measure. I therefore communicated in general terms the purport of my instructions on that head, with a further assurance that it was the intention of Government to open a most friendly and cordial intercourse with His Excellency had the measures been accomplished, the anticipation of which led to the present communication.

" The subject being now referred to His Highness the Viceroy of Egypt, without instructions from whom Ibrahim Pacha appears very averse to offer any reply to the letter of the Governor General, I entreat you, as a constituted authority of Government, to offer to His Highness's consideration the grounds on which the Governor General's letter was personally addressed to His Excellency Ibrahim Pacha, and the result which would have arisen from a cöoperation of the British armament, which must have tended to the establishment and security of the Government of the Pacha, had His Highness's views or intentions been directed to the possession of Arabia, or to the reduction of the only associated tribe of the allies of the Wahabee power which now remains to be subdued.

" I trust that His Highness's instructions on the subject, which

I have entreated you to explain, will enable His Excellency Ibrahim Pacha to form a suitable reply to the despatch of the Most Noble the Governor General; and that my detention at Yambo, the place now assigned for my residence till the return of His Excellency from the pilgrimage, will not be unnecessarily prolonged.

"Since my arrival at Medina I have not had the good fortune to obtain any information from which I could form an opinion of the policy which His Excellency Khuleel Pacha has been directed to pursue in the event of his obtaining possession of the capital of Senna. You are of course aware that there is not at present an Agent or Resident at Mocha, and consequently that the Government of Bombay cannot be informed of the alterations which are likely to take place with regard to the port of Mocha. As I shall probably touch at Mocha on my return, I shall feel particularly obliged by any information you may impart to me on this subject, which will no doubt essentially aid and assist me by directing my inquiries to the principal sources from whence possibly a correct opinion may be formed.

"I have the honour to be, &c.

"*Bir Alee, near Medina, 10th September 1819.*"

September 11th.—This afternoon a very unfortunate event took place. A convoy on its route from Yambo to Medina arrived within three miles of Bir Alee; one of the principal officers with the convoy, the son of the Chaia, being desirous to reach Medina as early as possible, separated from the guard and pushed on in advance, attended by five horsemen. At a narrow pass in the mountains they were attacked by a party of the banditti which infest these mountains. The Chaia's son was wounded severely through the knee, and one horseman shot through the breast; the other horsemen escaped and arrived at Bir Alee, stating that they had left the two men dead. The party which was ordered out to bring in the bodies of the two persons supposed to have been killed, found them in a miserable situation; they have been since removed into our camp. The indifference of the Turkish soldiery to the misfortunes of their comrades is fully elucidated by this conduct; they generally abandon to their fate those whom they imagine to be beyond recovery.

September 13*th*.—Mahomed Effendi (Mohurdar), brother to the wounded officer, arrived from Medina to visit his brother, and with instructions to alter the arrangement of our march. There not being a sufficient number of troops to form a guard, my destination has been altered to Yambo, whither the harem is to proceed to be embarked for Suez. His Excellency's stud is also to accompany. It consists of three hundred mares and horses, the choicest breeds of Arabia, which His Excellency has collected from the different tribes of those districts which he visited, who scarcely retain either horse or mare to propagate the species; those parts of Arabia will therefore for many years remain destitute of good horses, which will now be transferred in a great measure to Egypt, whither His Excellency has heretofore despatched a great number, independent of the number carried out of Arabia by the soldiery.

If any of the Arabs in the neighbourhood of our route had still in their possession a horse of good caste, the owner would not venture to bring the animal into our camp to offer it for sale, as he might expect that his horse would be seized, and then he must return on foot to his camp to be laughed at. The plan usually adopted in the purchase of horses is worthy of notice. If the purchaser sees a horse to his purpose he applies to the owner, who permits him to examine the animal, and in some instances where the horse is known to be of a particular breed, a regular register of his pedigree is produced; the purchaser then proposes the price, and names the sum; this is invariably replied to on the part of the owner by the monosyllable La (the negative Particle), on which the offer is increased, and so on till the avarice of the Bedouin is satisfied. There is something peculiarly original in this method of bargaining; the owner never exposes his expectations, or the value he sets on his goods till he has obtained a knowledge of the wants of the purchaser, and the utmost price which he can afford to give. These bargains generally occur with travellers or strangers. The barter which takes place between the Bedouins must needs be very circumscribed. The custom of fixing the value by proposing a certain number of camels as an equivalent is still very common.

The Damascus caravan of pilgrims on their route to Mecca reached Medina this morning. The Pacha of Shaam, Saleh Pacha (of three tails), is charged with the protection of the Hajees and the new covering for the Caaba. Ibrahim Pacha, who is also of the three tailed dignity, is charged with the safety of the caravan from hence to Mecca, he being Pacha of Jeddah and the holy land of Mahomed. I was anxious to form some estimate of the number of pilgrims who have arrived under the protection of the Pacha of Shaam, and to witness their approach to the holy city, but this could not be accomplished. The Pacha had in his retinue some pieces of cannon, for the purpose of firing salutes on certain occasions: a discharge of the cannon announced his arrival. I learned from the Turks who returned this evening from the city, as well as from my own servants who had been there for the purpose of visiting the shrine of the prophet, that the number of pilgrims is by no means considerable, and falls very short of the account which I had previously heard; it is stated that a great number perished last year on their return from the deficiency of water; this is assigned as the reason for the number this year not exceeding five hundred. The pilgrims who compose this caravan are those of Constantinople, Turkey in Asia, Damascus, &c. From such extensive and populous regions one would have expected to have seen a greater number of devotees. The Grand Seignor has directed all the reservoirs and wells in this route to be repaired and re-established, and which order has been this year in part executed. I did not hear that any persons had perished on the march.

Of the city of Medina I can afford but an imperfect description. Infidels are not permitted to enter this hallowed spot, and I obtained but a very imperfect view of the sacred city, which is situated in a hollow amidst the most barren rocky muntains. The walls and bastions are built with stone and lime, and the minarets are all plastered and whitewashed, which in this dreary situation renders them very conspicuous. There are three gates, the one the gate of Damascus, which is rather a citadel than a gate. On this fort there are several pieces of cannon mounted, and here the green flag is displayed on Fridays. The two other gates are those of Juman, and Misser or Egypt. Over each there are holes for three pieces of cannon. On these gates the red flag is exhibited on festivals. Within the city is an extensive garden in which there are dates, pomegranates, vines, &c., and a few vegetables. The fruits are good, and indeed the vegetables, particularly the bamia. The city is watered by a stream called Aiecoon Zarkeh; the water is esteemed good; there are also several wells. Independent of the tomb of the prophet, there are four others, sacred to Fatima, Omar, Aboobekar, and Ali. In the city there are also two mosques. There is one cady, and there are two mooftees, the one of the Hanifeite, and the other of the Shafeite sect, to expound the laws and doctrines. There are thirty colleges, or rather schools, for the education of youth. This year the sum expended by order of the Grand Seignor amounted to six hundred purses. This is said to have been laid out in the repairs of the tombs, mosques, and other sacred buildings. If the account rendered can be depended on, these must have been so frequently repaired and renewed that there can now scarely remain anything of antiquity, if we except the actual tomb of the prophet, which probably has remained untouched. All the inhabitants of Medina subsist on the donations which are annually sent by different persons who wish to have prayers offered up in their names. The Hajees also make suitable bequests. The Grand Seignor annually sends a large sum; in fact the Mahomedan world contributes to the support of these lazy, idle beggars, who, as they are rich, conceive they have a right to be arrogant, and to treat even their benefactors with contempt and disdain. In their houses they are said to fare sumptuously, although they are proverbial for their avarice. Providence has been bountiful towards this city in supplying it most abundantly with water; still a stranger is obliged to purchase every drink he may require, and to pay liberally at every shrine at which he offers up his prayers. The sums collected are divided in certain ratios after the arrival of the Hajees. The inhabitants of Medina pay no taxes. A correct account has been lately taken of the number of habitations, which amounted to six thousand; of this number one-half are in ruins. The population amounts to eight thousand souls.

To the north of Medina is an extensive date plantation and gardens which contain many inhabitants.

To the west is Bir Alee, now in ruins. There are several villages and date plantations in this valley, which extends into the mountains to the south-west.

The preparations for our march having been completed, it was determined that we should depart on the 15th; the ladies to precede the column, conveyed in their tukth-rewans, which are a very clumsy uncomfortable description of carriage, constructed with two long poles or beams placed parallel, in the centre of which a platform is fixed; over this a canopy is constructed, covered with cloth, and impenetrable to either vision or air. This machine is carried by two camels, the one placed in advance and the other in rear, whose head is generally poked under the body of the carriage to enable the brute to see his road; the ends of the poles are slung over the saddles of the camels.

These conveyances have been used to very great advantage for the conveyance of howitzers used on beds as mortars, and of other things which had not in themselves the means of transport on proper wheeled carriages; dispensing with the raised canopy, the howitzer was placed on the platform, and the camels tackled as above.

This however, would not answer with the common camel of Arabia, the animal being altogether too slight for so laborious an undertaking. The camels of Arabia are extremely fine animals for the conveyance of backloads, provided they are not over-burthened; they will out-march those of Egypt, being slighter and more active; they also can exist on the bushes which you find in the desert on each day's march, but this is not the case with the Egyptian camel, which is a very large, heavy animal, requiring a large portion of corn and forage, and incapable of moving at a quick pace.

Our escort consisted of some horsemen who were on their return to Egypt, and the remains of the Mugrabeen Bedouins proceeding to their homes; these latter receive no pay, and subsist by plunder. They drove with them the fruits of their labour, consisting of camels and horses of all ages and sizes, together with women, children, and slaves whom they had seized in the different sorties and pillages.

The Mugrabeens appeared very much discontented with the manner in which the Pacha had dismissed them after so arduous a campaign, in which they bore a great part of the fatigues, particularly in guarding convoys. His Excellency did not bestow a single dollar as bucksish on those unfortunate men who had followed his fortunes from the shores of the Mediterranean to the shores of the Persian Gulf. These men were particularly well adapted to this service, being themselves Bedouins and reared up in exactly the same habits as those of Arabia; they were equal to any fatigue, and could exist on any nourishment, either weeds, herbs, milk, or animals, that chance might throw in their way. They are generally more robust than the Bedouins of Arabia, and are said to be more courageous, but this I am inclined to attribute to their being better armed, and of course better acquainted with their use. Each man is mounted on an Arab horse, the appearance of which is certainly miserable, but as it is a blood animal, its performance exceeds the expectations which one would form on first sight. They generally ride on a camel, and lead their horse ready saddled; their muskets are very long, and the bayonet is a fixture; the butt of the musket is formed like that of a match-lock; the lock is, however, the same as that in use among the French, and the whole piece I imagine is either of French or German manufacture. Many of them have pistols and sabres also, but the musket is the arm which they appear to place most dependence on. They form in troops or teeps, and charge at full speed; they discharge their muskets, and, setting up a yell, dash on with their firelock, which they carry back-handed over their heads, both hands being employed with the muskets; the horse is impelled forward by the constant application of the shovel stirrup. No doubt a charge of this kind would prove very destructive against a body of camel cavalry, which, feeling the severity of one attack, would not be inclined to stand a second on such unequal terms, and thence might arise the idea of the Bedouin of Barbary being a much braver man than the Bedouin of Arabia.

September 15th.—Marched from Bir Alec at 7 A.M., our route westerly through the mountains. About two miles from Bir Alec we came to the spot at which the two Turks had been wounded a few days previously. Two mountains of very difficult ascent command this pass within pistol-shot. Here the Bedouins had been posted awaiting the arrival of any solitary traveller who might chance to pass, and whom they might be capable to overpower. Continuing our route through the valleys, as we advanced we found bushes of bauble more abundant, and the rocky mountains of a more considerable elevation. We arrived at 5 P.M. at a spot which was marked by a small white tower on the top of a mountain to the west, at the foot of which we found a deep well of good water. We encamped in an amphitheatre, which was thickly stocked with bauble trees and bushes.

September 16th.—Marched at 5 A.M.; continued our route through the mountains in the same valley. These mountains are high, rocky, and barren; in the valley are several bushes, the road gravelly and good; the mountains to the south-east impassable. We halted at 12 at a solitary well which afforded but a scanty supply of water, the demand for which became very pressing before evening.

September 17*th*.—Marched at 4 A.M., and continued our route through the valleys as yesterday; we reached Jodeidah at 12. It is a miserable village of huts built of stone; one part of the village is built up against the side of the mountain, but the lower village, which has several date gardens, lies in the hollows. The water here is good, but the water-melons, cucumbers, &c., which we procured, were not good. The sun does not shine on this valley more than three hours a day, which renders it a very unhealthy spot. The tribes which reside in the mountains, and who retain this pass, are the Misroo and Mimoon. They have made paths along the tops of the mountains where they can assemble a large force, and the entrance to their valley was once strongly defended; they are all armed with pistols, fuzils, &c. On the advance of Toossan Pacha they defended their valley so resolutely that he did not effect his passage without the loss of many men. We proceeded on to the village of Humrah, which we reached at 12 P.M., and here found a tolerable supply of water, which was soon sipped up by the camels, which had not been watered since we set out from Bir Alee.

September 18*th*.—Marched at 4 A.M. Almost every person had to complain of the loss of camels or baggage or horses. The Turks never place any guard or watch during the night, and during last night the thieves had been particularly active. We found the mountains and valleys nearly the same as heretofore. At 7 o'clock we crossed a hill from which we descended by a very rugged, difficult, rocky road, which here divides into two branches; the one turning off to the south runs to Mecca and Jeddah, and unites with that which leads from Humrah towards the above places; the other road is that which we followed to the west, and which led us to Bir-ul-Sultan, where we arrived at 11 A.M. The well was very deep, and full of good water. Immediately over it on a hill were the ruins of a mosque. We encamped in a small, flat, sandy plain, thickly stocked with baubel trees. The road to Bedree is to the south of this range. There the two caravans of pilgrims—the Egyptian and Damascus—

always join and proceed to Mecca. The one having arrived at its stage, a salute was fired and answered by the other, which served to communicate the intelligence.

September 19*th.*—Halted this forenoon to forage the camels. The Muggrabeen Bedouins were sent on in advance to enable us to proceed with the more ease in the afternoon. We marched at 3 P.M.; continued our route till daybreak, when we emerged from the hills and halted at Melha, the wells of which are brackish.

September 20*th.*—Marched from Melha. Hence the country assumes a new aspect, and opens into an extensive plain bounded to the west by the Red Sea. Arrived at Yambo at 10 A.M. It is a miserable Arab seaport. It is surrounded by a wall of stone badly cemented, and now tottering. This wall is a modern work, and appears to have been built in consequence of the old walls being too circumscribed to afford protection to all the inhabitants. The old walls and one of the gates still remain standing, but appear to have no claim to antiquity of structure, although Yambo is a very ancient port. The area encompassed by this new wall is sufficiently spacious to contain five times the number of houses; there consequently remain several waste spots which are appropriated for dunghills, burying-ground, and receptacles for dead horses and camels; the air is consequently impure.

The supply of water at Yambo is very precarious; it is procured by collecting the rain-water in deep covered pits, which, as they are badly constructed, and little attention paid to the pure state of the water when deposited, it is not to be expected that it would improve by keeping. The wells sunk in the town produce a water which emits as abominable a smell as the bilge-water of a ship. It has happened that rain has not fallen here for three successive years, in which case Yambo must have been nearly deserted. Within three or four miles of the town good water may be procured from wells, which are contiguous to the ruins of a fort which was thrown up by Toossan Pacha in the plain to cover his camp.

Yambo has been the depôt for the supplies of the Pacha's army, and the point at which it formed its rendezvous both by sea from Suez and Cossair, and by land from Suez, by which route the cavalry marched. It is twenty-four days' march from Suez. The supply of water on this route is precarious and scanty.

There is another town called Yambo situated a little to the southward, but inland. There water is abundant, and the gardens produce vegetables for the supply of the seaport. I did not visit this place, the weather being excessively sultry and my health much impaired. I at one time proposed to change the scene by removing to the other Yambo, supposing that the appearance of water and gardens would have been a recreation, but was dissuaded from this plan, being informed that the inland town was still more unhealthy than the seaport.

My stay at Yambo was rendered particularly unhappy by an attack of fever. In this forlorn situation I had neither medicines nor medical assistance. The courier returned on 19th October with the unpleasant intelligence of Mr. Salt's absence from Cairo, but as this man brought letters from His Highness Mahomed Ali Pacha for His Excellency, who had been for some time at Jeddah, I determined to embark on the first boat I could procure and proceed to Jeddah. This place I reached in an open boat in four days.

Although I arrived early in the forenoon of 27th I was unable to procure any accommodation on shore till the afternoon of the following day, and His Excellency's attention was so much occupied with the examination of the accounts of the Governor of Jeddah, whom he was about to displace, that he did not recollect that it was necessary some person should be directed to convey His Excellency's wishes as to the time it would be convenient for him to grant me an audience. I was therefore under the necessity of making known my anxiety to His Excellency, who received me on the evening of 29th. As usual an apology was offered for the omission of not having sent any person to receive me. Our conversation was not very interesting. His Excellency was surrounded by a number of persons connected with the Governor now in disgrace, and his inquiries were directed to the prices of rice, sugar, and piece-goods at Calcutta, and on which subject I unfortunately could not afford him much information. I ventured to urge a question on the subject of the reply from Cairo, to which His Excellency answered that at a future period he would be at leisure to converse on the subject. I intimated to His Excellency that it might be more convenient to him to nominate any of his ministers or officers through whom I might communicate, as hitherto I was unacquainted with the person through whom I should be at liberty to convey any solicitation to His Excellency. To this request he did not appear to attend.

On my return from His Excellency's house I was accompanied by two of his torch-bearers, natives of Cairo, who as they have been regularly educated in their profession, conceived they had the same right to exercise their assumed authority on the present occasion as though it was the Pacha himself who was proceeding in state. They had hardly issued from the gate when they commenced to disturb the unfortunate pilgrims and beggars who lay asleep in the streets on the bare ground, many without covering, and presenting the most wretched spectacle of misery. In fact every street in Jeddah was at this moment so crowded with people of different Mahomedan countries that it was difficult to pass from one street to the other even during the day.

The city, which is well built and contains many lofty and spacious houses, can scarcely afford shelter to the number of pilgrims and persons of more affluent circumstances; the indigent and those whose funds have been expended in prosecuting long and perilous journeys to accomplish this object of their faith, are constantly exposed to the greatest miseries. There are several encampments of this people on the outside of the town, and I would estimate the temporary accession of people requiring provisions at thirty thousand. This crowd is composed of Indians, who from the remotest parts find their way through Surat, Malabar, and Calcutta, some people from Sind, and many Arabs from Oman and the adjoining coast, who prefer the route of the Red Sea, as they can thereby unite temporal pursuits with religious duties. From the Eastern Isles there are a considerable number of Malay Mahomedans. A great number of Turks return by this route, viâ Cossair, to Cairo and Upper Egypt. Of the Barbary Arabs or Muggrabinees I perceived a great number also. Many days elapsed without a further communication, and I availed myself of an opportunity to visit the Chaia, to convey to him my wishes. He said he was totally unacquainted with the subject, but that the Pacha would certainly embark in a few days; that if he should hear any thing of the matter he would inform me. The Pacha having at this moment summoned the Chaia, I requested him to present my respects to His Excellency.

Since the period of His Excellency's arrival at Jeddah, after performing the pilgrimage, it presents a scene of confusion not to be described. The investigation of the governor's accounts involved many persons, who were variously tortured to extort confessions regarding the supposed peculations. The governor, Seyud Ali, was doomed to suffer many indignities.

The 16th having been nominated as the day of His Excellency's departure, I solicited another interview, which took place on the evening of 12th. His Excellency expressed some regret at the delay, which he said originated in his not being able to procure a scribe capable of drawing up an Arabic letter, but that he would order a further inquiry to be made on the morrow; that he intended to draw up a letter expressing his regret that the communication had not been made at an earlier period, which would have enabled him to unite in the views of the British Government.

His Excellency expressed his desire to send a suitable present with the letter, and in the selection of which he requested my opinion, remarking that in this situation it was difficult to procure any thing adapted to the occasion. My reply to His Excellency was that the value of the article sent on such occasions was not a matter of consequence, as the compliment was generally estimated by the manner in which it was conveyed, and the value of the article by the expression of friendship which accompanied it. His Excellency expressed a wish to send an Arab horse and mare, requesting me to take charge of them, and be the medium of presenting them to the Most Noble the Governor General, to which I of course assented. His Excellency expressed his intention of conferring a mark of favour on me, and said he should also send a horse for my acceptance, for which I returned my acknowledgments to His Excellency, who informed me that he had ordered a boat (buggalo) to be in readiness to convey me to Mocha.

As it was necessary that I should be acquainted with the reply of His Excellency, I requested that I might be favoured with a copy, which might become necessary in the event of accident, and in order to enable me to form a translation, to which His Excellency gave his consent.

On 14th of November the draft of the letter was sent to me, with a request that I would return it after perusal, and send the title and address of the Most Noble the Governor General. I complied by transmitting a copy from the letter in my possession in which the title Ushruf-ul-Ushruf forms a part. To this a very serious objection was started as appertaining solely to the Mahomedan prophet. To obviate difficulties and prevent cavil as to words, I remarked to the person who was sent to point out the objection that the title Umjud-ul-Umjud, &c., may be easily substituted. His Excellency canvassed this subject with much more warmth than good sense. To me the expression appeared inoffensive. The title of His Highness Abbass Meerza is nearly the same. Nuwab Ushruf, and the different modes of this root are used in a variety of forms to express nobility and pre-eminence in the system of letter-writing in vogue throughout the East, as well in the Arabic as the Persian language. His Excellency and his advisers argued on this point with each other till religious frenzy gained the ascendancy over their understandings. In this case all cavil and objection was obviated by the proposal of the introduction of an epithet conveying the same sense.

A visit from three or four of His Excellency's saises, who came to request a present or donation, was the only further intimation that reached me respecting the horses, which His Excellency had directed to be embarked on the boat in which it was intended I should proceed to Mocha. In this instance he had studiously avoided to do me the honour or pay me the compliment of permitting me to see the animals which he had specially requested me to be the medium of presenting, and regarding which he had consulted with me at the last interview, but on this subject I offered no remark.

One of His Excellency's domestics brought to my residence some parts of a set of horse furniture which he said he had been directed to deliver as an appendage to the horses intended for the Governor General, and that they had been sent in an open or loose state by the Treasurer. These consisted of a headstall, breastplate, and saddle-cloth, silver mounted and gilt, and a pair of stirrups of silver. On viewing the saddle-cloth it was impossible to avoid observing the tattered condition and ragged appearance which it presented, and which marked it to have been an useful appendage to His Excellency on many former occasions. It did not appear to me that in offering my opinion on a subject on which I had been previously consulted there could be any risk of offending against the rules of Turkish politeness, and of which I do not propose to plead a total ignorance. I directed the bearer to return in company with the person who was to convey a message to the Chaia on the subject, informing that minister " that I had deferred the acceptance of the saddle furniture till I should have an opportunity of conversing with him on the subject, and for which purpose I requested to be informed when and where I should have the honour of waiting on him." On the return of His Excellency's messenger the articles were given to him to be conveyed to the Treasurer till an explanation with the Chaia should take place. As the Chaia did not inform me when he would be at leisure to receive me, I had no opportunity of conversing with him.

His Excellency's Hukeem Bashee, who generally acted as interpreter, was then called upon to discover the motive or grounds for my offering an objection. I acquainted that gentleman with the circumstances, and requested him to convey to His Excellency my readiness to wait on him and offer my explanation personally. His Excellency preferred an explanation through the interpreter, and I offered the following: That the trappings were not a necessary accompaniment, and as they could not be procured in a new or fresh state, it was more politic they should be dispensed with. I authorised the interpreter, in the event of His Excellency requiring a further explanation, to offer my opinion "That articles which had been used could not be considered a suitable present to a nobleman filling so high an official situation under the British Government as the Marquis of Hastings now fills."

His Excellency directed the Hukeem Bashee to convey the following message to me:—" That as I had offered an objection on the subject of the trappings, His Excellency had ordered the horses to be disembarked, that the reply was annulled, and the letters ordered to be destroyed; and that His Excellency directed me to depart on the morrow in the boat which had been prepared to convey me to Mocha; that His Excellency on arriving at Cairo would address a letter to the Governor General, returning the sword which had been presented.

It appeared evident to me from His Excellency's deportment that he aimed at lessening the dignity of the British authorities in the eyes of his court and of the people of Jeddah, and that he wished to arrogate to himself a superiority, not an equality, to which latter title a Pacha could have no just claim. To the ceremony of presents a great weight is attached, equally as much as to titles; on declining to use a certain word on the plea of adherence to religious prejudice, it became politic to offer another version to evade cavil and litigation, or the appeance of an inclination to offend.

On the subject of the present I had already declined to offer an opinion, although frequently pressed to do so at the interview, and had the saddle-cloth and trappings been sent on board the boat, together with the horses, I could have had no further opinion to offer; but as the latter had been expressly sent to me, and in an open loose state to be viewed, I could form no conjecture than that an obstinate refusal to express my sentiments would have subjected me to the imputation of having publicly accepted and given my approbation to a present which certainly bore the interpretation of an intended slight.

I referred the matter to the Chaia or Minister and to the Treasurer, who appeared to me to be the proper persons, and through whom an alteration ought to have been effected without any further reference, particularly when the message was accompanied by a plausible excuse for the withholding of that part which appeared offensive. But the inclination to please did not exist in the bosoms of any of these persons. So long as their contempt was personally confined to myself I felt bound to appear insensible to it, but it was impossible for me to feign ignorance of a custom which is so well known to the meanest Turk.

Garments or vestments that have been worn are only offered to dependents or servants, and His Excellency would not presume to offer to his Minister or to his Silikdar any article which bore such traces.

To this message therefore there remained only one reply to offer; that under any other circumstances I should have accepted the accommodation of the buggalo; that I should now procure a vessel at my own expense to convey me to the destination I might now prefer, and at such time as would best suit my convenience.

Addressed the following letter :—

"To H. SALT, Esq., F.R.S.,
    Her Majesty's Consul General, &c., Egypt.

"SIR,—I regret that during my stay at Yambo or Jeddah as yet I have not had the good fortune to receive a reply to my former address, which was conveyed to Cairo by His Excellency's courier. On his return he delivered Mr. Pierce's letter, informing me of your absence. My stay at Yambo was rendered particularly unhappy by an attack of fever in so forlorn a situation. I therefore proceeded to Jeddah the instant I was able to repair on board a boat, and have not as yet been able to shake off this complaint.

"2. My reception at Jeddah was not flattering, and a considerable delay has taken place, for which an excuse was offered, that a scribe could not be procured who was capable of drawing up an Arabic letter.

"3. At my second interview, several days subsequent to my arrival, His Excellency expressed his intention to draw up a reply to the despatch of the Most Noble the Governor General, expressing his regret that the communication had not been made at an earlier period, which would have afforded him the happiness of uniting in the views and intentions of the British Government, and requested me to take charge of a horse and mare to be selected for the personal use of the Most Noble the Governor General, to whom he requested them to be presented. This I informed him I of course should endeavour to accomplish. I therefore considered His Excellency's determination as fixed.

"4. The reply was prepared and sent to me for perusal, with a request that I would send the title and address of the Governor General. I complied by transmitting a copy from the letter in my possession, in which the title of Ushruf-ul-Ushruf forms a part. To this a very serious objection was stated as appertaining only to the Mahomedan prophet; and to obviate difficulties and prevent cavil as to words, I remarked that the title Umjud-ul-Umjud might be easily substituted.

"5. His Excellency directed three horses to be embarked on the boat in which I was to proceed to Mocha; two were intended for the Most Noble the Governor General, and one as a present to myself. His Excellency did not, however, do me the honour or pay me the compliment to permit me to see the animals which he had specially requested me to present, and regarding which he had previously asked my opinion; but on this subject I offered no remark.

"6. As a necessary appendage to the horses intended to be presented to the Governor General, His Excellency directed his Treasurer to send a set of gilt trappings. These were accordingly brought to me in an open or loose state to be viewed, and, as the saddle-cloth and other parts appeared much tattered and worn, I directed them to be returned to the Treasurer till such time as I should have an opportunity of consulting with His Excellency's Chaia, of whom I requested the honour of an interview, which however, has never taken place.

"7. His Excellency expressed much dissatisfaction at the return of the trappings, to which I offered, through the medium of His Excellency's Hukeem Bashee, who acted as interpreter, the following reply: That the trappings were an unneccessary accompaniment, and that as they could not be procured new, it was more politic they should be dispensed with, as articles which had been used could not be considered a suitable present to a nobleman holding so high an official situation under the British Government as the Marquis of Hastings now fills.

"8. His Excellency directed an answer to be conveyed through the same person, that as I had declined to convey the trappings which he had directed to accompany the horses, they should be ordered to be disembarked, the letters should be destroyed, and that I should be in readiness to depart on the morrow on the boat which had been prepared to convey me to Mocha. That His Excellency would, on his arrival at Cairo, procure a scribe to address a suitable letter to the Governor General, to whom he purposed to return the sword which had been presented.

"9. With regard to my personal conduct on these points I shall offer my remarks. I considered myself entitled to be informed of the subject of His Excellency's reply, as the instructions under which I have acted pointed out a certain line of conduct to be adopted under certain circumstances which might arise. Moreover, His Excellency had stated to me his want of confidence in the abilities of his Arabic scribe, and had sent the draft of the letter to me for perusal; and with regard to the version of the title, it is that used on all occasions, and to which I had never heard any objection offered. In this case all cavil and objection was obviated by the introduction of an epithet conveying the same sense.

"10. With regard to the ostensible reason of His Excellency's displeasure and chagrin, I must inform you that His Excellency had expressly consulted with me and solicited my opinion on the fitness of the present of which he requested me to be the medium of presentation. I cannot therefore imagine that I trespassed on the rules of politeness and good breeding in offering the opinion which I have narrated in the 6th paragraph.

"11. The instructions which I have received for the guidance of my conduct directed me to inform you particularly of the nature of my reception. I shall therefore detail to you the leading features. I set out from Ul-Ahsa under an assurance that I should reach His Excellency's camp within ten days. After a painful march of thirty-five days I arrived within a stage of His Excellency, then at Anizeh. He was perfectly aware of my being in company with the Kuftun Agasee, but neither would he await my arrival, nor did he take any precaution to ensure my more speedy junction. His Excellency's not having authorized any person to communicate with me, and the state of Arabia at that moment, obliged me to proceed on to Medina, which might have been obviated, and my return to Bussorah effected with ease.

"12. My arrival at Bir Alee was not marked by any public compliment, to which an evident disinclination was evinced. His Excellency was, however, affable in conversation, and honoured my residence with his presence: but on discussing the principal or only question, which in fact should never have arisen

His Excellency's deportment was so extremely self-opinionated, that I was obliged to consent to his referring a subject to Cairo, which had been solved before I set out from Ul-Ahsa, and which had already occasioned a delay of more than two months, as you will perceive by referring to the dates of my two communications.

"13. On my arrival at Jeddah I naturally expected that some person of His Excellency's court would have been deputed to receive me, or wait on me after my landing; this was, however, studiously avoided, and my request, frequently urged, that I might be made acquainted with the Minister or Secretary, through whom I may communicate with His Excellency, has never been acceded to. I have therefore in general had more communication with Quwasses, Saises, and Farases, than with any other persons attached to His Excellency.

"14. I have been thus prolix in my explanation that you may be the better prepared to elucidate these occurrences to His Highness Mahomed Alee Pacha. On your representation of the circumstances it is probable he will feel inclined to view the deportment of His Excellency in the light it deserves, and to express his disapprobation in such terms as will anticipate the remonstrances which that line of conduct must naturally draw forth.

"I have the honour to be, &c.

"*Jeddah, 14th November* 1819."

November 16*th*.—On the morning of 16th His Excellency embarked under a salute of all the artillery both afloat and ashore, from which it may be inferred that the Turks of Egypt are not unmindful of the importance attached to public compliments, or as they denominate such shows, fantasia. On the morning of 17th His Excellency sailed direct for Cossair without any intention of visiting Yambo; on this occasion the salute was repeated till the ships were clear of the harbour. The joy expressed by the inhabitants of Jeddah on the departure of the Pacha, and their release from tyranny, was not only manifested in their countenances, but even now publicly expressed in all societies. Previous to his departure he had appointed Rais Hajee Hussun, who formerly had been Commodore or Sirdar of the fleet, to officiate in the place of the late Governor, Seyud Allee, who had been removed from the government on the plea of appropriating to his private use the profits which he derived from trade at Jeddah. Such are the rules of Turkish equity that the Pacha considers himself entitled to the money earned by this man in trading to India in his own ships, and with his own capital, arguing that as a servant the master alone had a right to the profits. His Excellency's katibs were assisted by the bludgeons of the Quwasses in adjusting the accounts of the Seyud, who saw himself stripped of ten years' earnings in as many days, and turned adrift a beggar, in the very city of which he had been once the Governor.

On the morning of 18th I had the pleasure to receive a visit from the new Governor, accompanied by Arabee Jilanee, and several merchants who had been in the habits of intercourse with the English. They freely expressed their regret at not being able to evince their inclination to show me any attention during the presence of the Pacha, who, as they said, had never intimated his wishes, and whose silence they construed into a prohibition. At all events they did not wish to manifest any peculiar intercourse, lest the jealousy of the Pacha should be roused. Rais Hussun had been to Calcutta and Bombay in command of the Pacha's ships, and expressed his gratitude for the kind treatment he had experienced. Arabee Jilanee is a man whose family have rendered peculiar service to the English, particularly during the expedition to Egypt, when their interest with the Shureef of Mecca enabled them to procure large supplies of cattle and provisions for the fleet. The ascendancy of the Turks at the present moment renders such services entirely subservient to their caprice, and, however well inclined the individual may be to forward the interests of his former friends, it appears that the dread of the Pacha's pistols and bludgeons has a more decided effect than British gold, as, notwithstanding all my entreaties, I could not procure a messenger to convey my letters to Cairo, and was obliged to be very circumspect in the manner of forwarding them.

I determined to remain at Jeddah in the hope of receiving a reply from Mr. Salt previous to the arrival of a vessel from India, which route alone now remained open, it being impossible to communicate with Bussorah, or return by any other route; indeed, so hazardous an attempt would appear unnecessary, and offer no prospect of public benefit: first, if it were possible for the causids to return from Rus to Bussorah, Kutteef, &c., the Government must be already apprised of the failure of the mission, and, on the other hand, if these men failed in the attempt, I could not naturally expect to succeed; secondly, the period of my arrival in the Persian Gulf must be long subsequent to the conclusion of the expedition.

Addressed a letter * to the Honorable Mr. Elphinstone, Governor and President in Council of Bombay, detailing the foregoing particulars.

Having for the present brought to a conclusion the affairs of this mission, I shall endeavour to collect, from the notes which I have made on former occasions, and the narratives of the best informed actors on the stage of His Excellency's late campaigns, as correct a sketch of the proceedings of the Turks in Arabia as can be now obtained, by comparing the different accounts of their battles as related by the most intelligent officers and persons concerned in these exploits; commencing with a brief account of Ibrahim Pacha, who is the eldest son of the Viceroy of Egypt, by a widow, the sister of Mustuffa Bey, of Drama, an officer of distinction. It is said that Ibrahim was born a few months after the marriage of his parents, which gives rise to a story that he is only the adopted son of Mahmud Ali. He passed one year as a hostage at Constantinople, from whence he was removed to the

* This letter, dated Jeddah, 18th November 1819, has been forwarded to Calcutta, vide Appendix B.

situation of Dufturdar at Cairo, in which office he was esteemed intelligent in the affairs of the revenue, but extremely intemperate, and cruel to the persons employed under him. On the departure of Mahmud Ali Pacha on his last campaign with the Mamlúkes in Egypt, Ibrahim Bey commanded 300 cavalry, and obtained the reputation of a brave soldier. This affair ended in the murder of all those Mamlúkes who fell into the hands of the Pacha, and closed with a general massacre of all residing at Cairo, and in the villages of Upper Egypt, whither Ibrahim Bey was soon despatched to collect the revenues, and dispose of the villages to the new farmers of the customs, accompanied by a number of Copts as clerks, who managed to embezzle large sums. From this duty he returned to Cairo, where he was appointed to command the army destined to drive the Mamlúkes beyond Ibrim. This duty he performed, and returned to Asna with a number of prisoners and others who accepted the protection of the young Bey. Here they were separated and placed in the houses of different persons in the confidence of the young Bey, who shortly after sent an order from Cairo to Mahomed Effendi (son of the present Chaia of Ibrahim, and at this moment his Mohurdar) to destroy every individual. The Effendi obeyed the orders of his master, commencing the slaughter with his own hand. Subsequent to these transactions, in 1809, he was nominated Governor General of Upper Egypt, retaining the situation of Dufturdar. During his government, under his father's directions, he enhanced the revenues, and expended large sums for the improvement and the increase of cultivation, but all his acts were marked by an extreme severity and cruelty of disposition. On one occasion the young Bey ordered a Copt to be roasted on a spit; on another a Copt charged with embezzlement was placed by his orders in a heap of chopped straw saturated with oil; this heap was set on fire by Khoja Suleeman, then a Quwass in his service. Unfortunately these cruelties have not been confined to persons guilty of misdemeanours, but on several occasions have been extended to the domestics of his family. Were I to relate the many inhuman instances of butchery which have been exposed to my knowledge, accompanied by a detail of the minutest circumstances, and the names of the persons concerned, the catalogue would swell to an enormous size.

In 1813 Ibrahim Beg was created a Pacha of Two Tails, and was appointed to Girge. The cruelty of his disposition is said to have been checked at this moment by the responsibility of his situation, and the hope of future preferment, which appear to have operated very sensibly on his conduct. He had been much addicted to the joys of Bacchus, and in general enjoyed himself after the European fashion, with his bottle and glass placed on a table, while he reclined on a chair. On these occasions, however, he observed the strictest secrecy.

In 1815, he was appointed to the command of the army destined to penetrate into the interior of Arabia. The first troops who placed themselves under his orders were volunteers, but the number not proving sufficient, an order was issued by the advice of Ibrahim* (then his Chaia) to prevent any man from receiving his discharge, and obliging the whole of the troops to serve. The next step was an alteration in the saddles of the cavalry, substituting that in use anong the Muggrabine or Barbary Bedouins for the heavy Mamlúke saddle of Cairo; those were again replaced by the saddles of Romelia, which were eventually disused, and those of the fashion of Bagdad substituted. Each horse-soldier was obliged to supply himself with a camel for the transport of his baggage, and on which he was occasionally to ride, the Egyptian horse being unable to undergo much fatigue, and his tardy pace rendering him an unequal match for the Arab. It was necessary at all times to have the horses as fresh as possible. However, as the Government bore no part of these expenses, the troops murmured against the Pacha for exposing them to unprecedented expenses.

His Excellency having superintended the embarkation of the infantry, by the route of Cossair, for Yambo, returned to Cairo,

---

* This man subsequently absconded, and was replaced by the present Chaia, Suleeman Agha.

where he arranged his affairs with his father the Viceroy; and leaving his cavalry near Cairo in readiness to follow, only two hundred in the first instance were to proceed by land by the route of Suez to Yambo, where His Excellency arrived by the route of Cossair, attended only by a few Mamlúkes. On entering the holy land of Mahomed, His Excellency determined to renounce the joys of Bacchus, and destroyed the whole of the stock he had brought with him from Cairo, previous to his departure for Medina.

The Pacha ordered his camp to be formed at Melca, near Yambo, where the troops were detained forty days, awaiting a supply of camels, &c., from the Bedouin tribe of Jehina, which together with the tribes of Mymoon, Aoof, and Misroo, occupy the mountains, extending from Medina towards Yambo, and to the southward towards Mecca. He was eventually obliged to send a force against the first of those tribes, which seized one thousand of their camels, brought off two thousand of their sheep, and killed one hundred and fifty of the tribe. Of the Pacha's party two only were wounded. From this circumstance some estimate may be formed of the inequality of the combatants.

The army, then consisting of two hundred Turkish cavalry, two hundred Muggrabine or Barbary Bedouin horsemen, and nine hundred infantry, with three pieces of cannon, was ordered to move towards Henekah, and was joined by Aoozoon Ali's party, consisting of four hundred good cavalry, which heretofore had formed a separate command under their leader, a very distinguished officer, who had been left for the protection of Medina, with some other troops on the return of Toossun Pacha to Egypt. The Pacha's force had lost nearly four hundred men during its stay at Melca, which, as well as Yambo, proved a very unhealthy station. After remaining twenty-five days at Henekah, the Pacha detached a force against the tribe of Hurub, from whom he took one thousand five hundred camels; his soldiers brought off six thousand sheep, and a large quantity of dates.

Fearing the severity of those marauding attacks, many of the Bedouin Sheiks proposed to join the Pacha. Having united with those Arabs, he sent another detachment against the tribe of Aootibah, occupying the desert between Deriah and Mecca, but they, having gained intelligence of his intention, betook themselves to flight, drawing off their flocks and camels. Seventeen persons fell into the hands of the enraged Pacha, who commenced a slaughter of these unfortunates with his own sabre. This failure had nearly proved fatal to the Turks, who suffered the greatest miseries on their return, from the want of water and provisions, of which they had anticipated a superabundant supply from the pillage of the tents of the Bedouins, who, however, had filled up the wells, and destroyed everything they could not carry off.

The Pacha on his return to Henekah received the intelligence of his being appointed a Pacha of Three Tails by the title of the Pacha of Jeddah, in consequence of the death of his brother Toossun. It became necessary to return to Medina to receive the pelisse and publish the firman. On his return to Henekah, the Sheiks of the Anizeh tribe with many others met him, and mutual assurances were pledged; he therefore formed a magazine at this place.

The next enterprise was against the Arabs of Jubul Chumber. For this purpose he formed a detachment of six hundred Turkish cavalry, intended as a rear-guard, to force into action a body of one thousand Bedouin cavalry, and five thousand Bedouins mounted on camels, composed from those tribes which had attached themselves to him. As the Bedouins led the van, they had two hundred killed, and three hundred wounded; they lost a vast number of their horses and camels; of the Turks there were only five killed and ten wounded. The Turks gained but little solid advantage by this. If it added another terror to the name of the Pacha, it proved to the Bedouins they had been duped most egregiously.

At the representation of the Arab Sheikhs the Pacha ordered Aoozoon Alee with a part of his force and two pieces of cannon in advance to Maweeah, to overawe the Wahabee party, which had commenced attacking the camps of those Bedouins now associated with the Pacha. The Sheikh of the tribe of Mootair (Dewys), situated to the east of Anizeh, sent to the Pacha to propose a meeting at Maweeah. His Excellency departed, and on the way received the intelligence of an action between Aoozoon Alee's force and the Wahabees, who were completely defeated on the spot mentioned in the journal of 2nd September. The Pacha only arrived in time to put to death the prisoners who fell into the hands of the conqueror, and thereby increased the number of ears which His Excellency wished to send to Cairo as an offering to His Highness. The transport of heads being attended with difficulty, ears in pairs were substituted. The number of slaughtered Wahabees is reported to have exceeded the number of Aoozoon Alee's troops; and this day decided the fortune of Abdoolah, who fled to Rus, and thence by Anizeh to Deriah, and did not appear again in the field.

The Pacha now assembled his whole force at Maweeah. Having received some reinforcements, it amounted to fourteen hundred infantry, six hundred cavalry, eight pieces of cannon, one howitzer, and one mortar; with one hundred artillerymen, to which may be added four or five hundred Mugrabine infantry. He despatched an officer to order the cavalry from Cairo to join the army.

The Sheikh of Mootair sent his son to compliment the Pacha on the late victory, and, matters being arranged, this Sheikh joined the Pacha, and was received with every mark of distinction. The motives which induced this Sheikh to join against Abdoolah was a feud or hatred arising from the latter having murdered twelve Sheikhs or elders of the tribe, and relatives of the present Sheikh. Camels and assistance of every description becoming more abundant, the Pacha commenced bringing forward his stores and supplies, and prepared for the seige of Rus. His Excellency during this respite made a forage on one of the petty tribes included in the general name under the tribe of Anizeh. The reason assigned was that this tribe had been ordered to collect and join the Pacha, and for which eight days had been allowed. This period proved too limited in consequence of the distance, but to this excuse, which is said to have been just, no attention was paid. His Excellency met the tribe on its march to join him, notwithstanding which he deprived them of the whole of their flocks of sheep, which he divided among the troops lately arrived from Cairo.

His Excellency having put his force in march for Rus, arrived before that town, which he said he was determine to carry before he would permit his camp to be pitched or his cavalry to dismount from their horses. Accordingly the Topchee Bashee was directed to advance the artillery within eighty paces of the walls, and to commence a cannonade on the strongest boorj, or bastion. The troops not being covered, and the artillerymen being exposed to a heavy fire of musketry, the slaughter of the Turks exceeded tenfold that of the besieged, who defended the city with spirit. For three days His Excellency cannonaded this boorj and the adjoining wall, which was eventually reported to be breached. The assault was ordered, and, to enable the infantry to pass the ditch, fascines were ordered to be made from date branches, and a number of sacks were filled with straw. Six hundred infantry were selected for the assault. These men threw themselves into the ditch, from which they could not ascend. The fascines, &c., had proved insufficient; the enemy opened a destructive fire from the walls, and the Pacha, attended by his Mamlúkes, shot every soldier who attempted to retreat. Thus the unfortunate infantry suffered a dreadful loss. Those who had been killed were denied the right of burial by an order from His Excellency, who was enraged at the failure. The siege of Rus was prolonged for three months and a half, during which time the Wahabees of Rus displayed more science than the Turkish General. The batteries formed by the Pacha cost fifty-two thousand German crowns; four hundred camel-loads of musket ammunition were expended in firing into the town; thirty thousand charges of ammunition were uselessly thrown away by the artillery. Stages were erected of date trees of such a height as to enable the soldiery to fire into the town; the cannon were advanced to the very edge of the ditch; two assaults were attempted, in which the Turks were repulsed, and lost a great number of men. The Pacha, unable to effect or accomplish this task, was finally obliged to enter into terms, and raise the siege. None of his troops were allowed to enter into the city. Whatever they required was to be purchased of the inhabitants, and Rus was to remain in a state of neutrality till the fate of Anizeh should be determined. In this affair the Turks had nine hundred killed, one thousand wounded, and were reduced to the greatest distress. The besieged lost only fifty killed, and seventy wounded. Two convoys conveying large supplies of provisions had the good fortune to arrive in safety, which proves a want of vigilance on the part of the Turks, as the country is a perfect flat. They assert that the yellow earth of which the walls were composed was of such an adhesive quality that their balls took no effect.

His Excellency then turned his attention to Kabreh, which place surrendered after a day's siege. From thence His Excellency marched against Anizeh; Abdoolah had left a garrison here, but having himself retired to Deriah, the Sheikhs of the town of Anizeh entered into terms, on which only the citadel or fort was cannonaded; the magazine which was formed in one of the boorjes blew up, and afforded an easy entrance. The garrison capitulated, and was allowed to depart with arms and baggage. This affair took up five days.

Boreidah was then besieged, and reduced on the third day. Ibn Jilan was the Sheikh of this town. This man is reported to be one hundred and twenty years of age. His counsel heretofore was reported to have been of great weight with the Wahabee party; being now old and infirm, he was unable to make a stand against the Pacha. The Wahabees every day became more dispirited, and Abdoolah's retreat to Deriah, where he remained shut up and inactive, added to their dismay; all the villages in this district surrendered. Here the Pacha remained for two months, awaiting reinforcements to enable him to proceed against Shakrah; having arrived before this place, on the second day he commenced to cut down the date plantations, which induced the inhabitants to separate their interests from the garrison, which was obliged to surrender; leaving their arms and baggage in the fort, they were permitted to depart. Here the Pacha remained inactive for three months, awaiting reinforcements and supplies.

He next moved to Deroma, which was then in a very flourishing state. On the fourth day this place was assaulted. The Turks were at the first repulsed, but carried the town; three hundred of the garrison took shelter in a house, and eventually were permitted to depart without arms, under the command of their chief, named Saood, the brother of Abdoolah's mother. Here the Pacha's temper appears to have returned to its usual bent; for seven days the soldiers were employed in slaughtering the inhabitants of this town, and the usual reward of five German crowns for every pair of ears was granted on this occasion. Many of the soldiers had an opportunity of filling their purses without their courage being put to the test. The Pacha himself was as expert in discharging his pistols as the meanest soldier.

These affairs were brought to a close in the beginning of February 1818. The season was particularly cold, and several heavy falls of rain had taken place about this time.

His Excellency prepared for the attack of Deriah, and ordered up the reinforcements which were on the route to join him; his force now consisted of two mortars, one Swedish carronade, and one howitzer, four pieces of cannon (12 pounders), and five Turkish guns, one hundred and fifty gunners, and two hundred pioneers, twenty-one artificers, eleven miners; his infantry amounted to a total of four thousand three hundred, of which one thousand seven hundred and twenty-five were Arnaoots, and the remainder Turks, the Mugrabine or Barbary infantry amounted to one thousand three hundred men. The Pacha had a corps of Turkish cavalry of eight hundred and fifty men, Aoozoon Ali's corps amounted to four hundred, and Roshwan Agha's to three hundred; to this add Barbary horse, four hundred:—total one thousand nine hundred and fifty.

Cavalry,	Pacha's Turks and Arnaoots	850
,,	Aoozoon Ali's	400
,,	Roshwan Agha's	300
		1,550
,,	Barbary	400
	Grand Total	1,950
Infantry,	Arnaoots	1,725
,,	Turks	2,575
		4,300
,,	Barbary	1,300
	Grand Total	5,600

The attack of Deriah * was commenced from the north end or village of Fyzel, which consisted of gardens interspersed with houses, and covered by a wall and boorjes. This was carried at the end of seven days, when Abdoolah's force was obliged to retire within the wall which separated the village of Fyzel, or Jenein-ul-Fyzel, from the two greater divisions of the town of Deriah. The Pacha rested here some days, which gave leisure to the enemy to strengthen themselves in this new position, which cost the Pacha eventually seven months' labour. An accident of a serious nature occurred. The Pacha's magazine blew up, and the artillery remained without ammunition for nearly two months. The villages in the neighbourhood of Deriah, finding the siege prolonged, prepared to throw off the yoke, and the troops were distributed to keep them in check, which drew off so large a proportion that this extensive place could not be invested or inclosed by the remainder. The Pacha found himself obliged to attempt the assault, which

---

* Refer to Journal, 13th August.

he directed against the side of Tarefa. Fortunately for him, the enemy had expected this attack on the opposite side, of Seille, and there prepared to resist. The Pacha's troops advanced and gained Tarefa without firing a shot, which was a most fortunate circumstance, as the greater body of his cavalry passed through the ravine. The resistance on the side of Seille was more obstinate. This town held out three days, but, the assailants being more numerous, they eventually succeeded. When the Turks gained possession of the village of Fyzel many of the Arabs of Deriah deserted the city, and never again returned to it. From that period Abdoolah's force became very weak. At the moment of this last assault there remained with him only two thousand of the four thousand who originally resisted the attack of the Turks. Abdoolah was now obliged to retire to the only place which still remained to him, the citadel of his family on the side of Tarefa, in which he shut himself up with two hundred men, the remains of his force. In this place he stood a bombardment of three days, when he requested a parley.

On visiting the Pacha he requested terms, a pardon for the troops who still had remained faithful to him, the same for his brothers and family at large, the preservation of the city, and the safety of his own person. The Pacha's deportment throughout this interview is represented as extremely haughty. To Abdoolah he presented his hand, who kissed it, as a mark of submission, although as yet not entirely fallen. The terms offered by the Pacha were the pardon of the troops, and of his brothers, and their families; with respect to the city, no terms would be promised, and as to the personal safety of Abdoolah, Ibrahim Pacha would only pledge his word for his safety till the period of his arrival at Cairo.

Abdoolah returned to his citadel, to brood over these melancholy prognostics of his future doom. On 4th September 1818 he delivered himself into the hands of the Pacha.

Abdoolah and his family prepared for their journey to Egypt, whither they were despatched. Of the fate of Abdoolah we have had accounts in India. One of his sons, who clearly foresaw the misery which awaited the whole party, determined to extricate himself, and effected his escape during the march. His absence was not discovered till there remained no trace of the route he had pursued. Some said he went to the north, others that he had fled to the south, and joined some Bedouins on the confines of Yemen, who still retained a friendship for the Wahabees. I made frequent inquiries respecting this man, but could obtain no information. The Bedouins professed total ignorance of the subject, lest they should be supposed to be acquainted with the place of his retreat. The Turks never spoke of the circumstance, as it had been hushed up, and never reported to Muhumud Ali Pacha. Ibrahim denied it as he did not wish to be detained in the country in pursuit. Whenever the subject was introduced in private confab, this man was represented as a fool or an idiot, to lessen the consequence attached to the circumstance, which to me appeared of great weight.

Had Abdoolah absconded from Deriah and the members of his family separated, the Turks would have been obliged to remain in Arabia, and to separate into small bodies in pursuit of them. Some few would have escaped as the Turks would have been exhausted. The whole family must have been well aware of their impending fate the instant they fell into the hands of the Pacha. The nominal fool appears to have been the only wise man of the family.

To this opinion an objection is started that the members of that family could not have expected protection from the Bedouins of Arabia from the moment that their power ceased, as the Bedouins were only constrained followers of that faith, or at most, merely adhered to it only so long as the sect was powerful, or followed it through the hope of plunder, of which peculiar trait Saeed took constant advantage, and seldom permitted them to remain inactive, the neglect of which appears to have operated to the injury of Abdoolah's cause, particularly in shutting himself up in forts and towns, in place of hanging on the rear of the Turks and cutting off their supplies. But the greatest fault he appears to have committed was in offering them battle at Maweeah.

The pillars of the Wahabees' faith having been removed from Arabia, the Bedouins of Nedjed, and all those whom I have seen, universally proclaimed themselves of the Soonee creed. They are particularly punctual in their devotions, and never omit to perform the stated prayers, even on the longest marches, and under the most severe privations. A strange contrast, when compared with the more enlightened Turk, who never allows religion or prayers to interfere with his comfort or ease.

I have already remarked that at Manfooah, and Riaz, I met with some persons who still avowed themselves to be of that faith; these were the remains of the former inhabitants of Deriah, and not Bedouin Arabs, their number was inconsiderable, and I have since learned that the Kashif had meditated the destruction of the whole during our detention at that place. The dubious fate of the Saleemiah party prevented him from carrying his intentions into execution. When that party joined he moved off with all possible expedition in pursuit of the Pacha, under constant apprehension of being left to his fortune, and being surrounded and cut off; the Pacha having deserted us and set off for Rus, and thence to Medina, contrary to his promise.

Ibrahim having obtained possession of Deriah entered the citadel and house of Abdoolah with a few confidential servants. None of the family were permitted to carry off any moveables; and he no doubt expected to find some valuables, in which I believe he was disappointed. It was supposed that a vast collection of books had been amassed; few were found, other than Korans, which were sent in triumph to Medina to be examined by the doctors of divinity, ere they were allowed to be read.

The soldiery were allowed to enter the city and select quarters for themselves, pillage, and ill treat the few inhabitants who remained to take care of their houses and gardens. The

Pacha seized the persons of those whom he suspected to have secreted their money and property, and by various tortures and stratagems he obtained large sums.

One artifice to discover the monied men is worthy of notice.* All those lands which were supposed to have belonged at a former period to mosques or other religious institutions, he restored to persons of the Soonee faith, who were to preach that creed; and he proposed to restore the other gardens, date plantations, and lands to the rightful owners, without injury, provided they would ransom them. This some few agreed to, on which the Pacha seized them, and enforced the payment of the sum, alleging they must have the amount in their possession, or they would not have acceded to the offer. He was well aware in the first instance that the orders of the Porte directed the total destruction of Deriah, and that he could only defer compliance till the order was issued publicly, on which occasion the unfortunate inhabitants again proposed to save their property and the means of a future existence; the Pacha took advantage of this, and after extorting from many, he totally destroyed Deriah by cutting down every date tree in its neighbourhood, his soldiers burning every beam and stick in the houses of the inhabitants.

His Excellency's further proceedings, till the period of his departure from Jeddah, are detailed in the journal.

During my detention at Jeddah awaiting an opportunity to return to India, Khuleel Pacha visited that place. He is a Pacha of Two Tails under the orders of Muhmud Ali, and had been sent

---

* It was probably to these occurrences that the Imam of Muscat alluded in his conversation in May 1819, although he was not then aware of the particulars. The Persians on my arrival at Bushire told a very different story. The former was anxious to render the character of the Pacha as odious as possible; the latter extolled his disinterestedness in replacing the Beni Khalid tribes in the sovereignty of Ul-Ahsa, suppressing the circumstances which induced the Pacha so to do; the Persians were happy even to deceive their own judgments in thus making a favourable representation, which, should it be realized, would afford them an access to Mecca and Medina.

over in command of an army of two thousand five hundred Turks and Arnaoots, to reinforce Ibrahim, who had written for further assistance at the period that the siege of Deriah was protracted. This Pacha did not arrive till subsequent to the fall of Deriah; his services in that quarter could not be required, and as the troops had been sent across the Red Sea at a considerable expense, Muhmud Ali determined to employ them against the Arabs of Aboo-Arish, who had subverted the government of Thehama, and of a part of Yemen. Comfida, Loheia, and many places on the coast fell into the hands of the Turks; they obtained possession of many places in the interior, and during this Pacha's stay at Jeddah Muhmud bin Muhumud, the last chief of the Yemenee Wahabees, was made a prisoner and brought in chains to Jeddah, from whence he was shipped off for Egypt. The Wahabee party in Yemen and Thehama being reduced, Muhmud Ali entered into a negotiation with the Imam of Sennaā, to whose father the sovereignty of those places now rescued from the adherents of the Wahabee, had formerly been subject. The present Imam was happy to accede to a proposal which would again restore to him a territory which he himself could not have reclaimed, and which for many years had been in a state of insurrection. The terms concluded were the restoration of all places in the interior which had belonged of right to the former Imam. The Turks were to evacuate Comfida, Loheia, and the seaports which they had blockaded, and to desist from all further hostilities. The Imam of Sennaā agreed to pay Muhmud Ali one lac of dollars a year as tribute; this was claimed by the Pacha on two grounds; first, he alleged that former Imams had been tributary to the Grand Seignior and had either paid this tribute in money or in coffee, through the Sultans of Egypt; secondly, he had restored, after an expensive warfare, nearly a whole province which had not for many years paid any revenue to the Imam of Sennaā. The Imam allowed the second proposition, and was happy to be released from his apprehensions of the views of the Turks, whose approach seemed to threaten his independence, and who were nearly as obnoxious to him as the Wahabees. Khuleel Pacha withdrew the remains of his troops in a miserable, sickly state, to Mecca, where he is to be stationed ; he occasionally visits Jeddah.

Jeddah.—On the afternoon of 23rd January I was delighted to see an English vessel approach Jeddah; she proved to be the cruiser " Prince of Wales," which had passed up to Cossier, and now on her return to Mocha. It was somewhat unlucky that she had not touched on her way up, as it would have afforded me an opportunity to communicate with Mr. Salt, from whom I had not received a reply, although the persons through whom my letters had been forwarded, informed me of their having been delivered, and many letters from Ibrahim Pacha, written subsequent to his arrival at Cairo, had reached Jeddah.

It would have been highly gratifying to me to have learned His Highness Muhmud Ali Pacha's opinion on the proceedings at Jeddah, and in what light he had viewed the conduct of his son, but I could not assure myself of the practicability of reaching Mocha by another conveyance before the sailing of the " Prince of Wales." I determined not to lose so favourable an opportunity of returning to Bombay, to report thus far the result of my mission, conceiving that the arrangement of the points in discussion could not be entrusted to a person better situated for adjusting them than the Consul General.

The " Prince of Wales" arrived at Mocha on the 11th of February, after a most tempestuous passage ; we were detained awaiting the reply to the despatch* which had been sent up to the Imam of Sennaá till the 28th March, when we set sail for India, and reached Bombay on the 8th of May.

On my arrival I learned that the last letter received from me was that written from Ul-Ahsa. Of the pilgrims who had at-

---

* This letter had been delivered at Mocha on 25th December ; the journey to Sennaá is to be accomplished in 13 days, provided no impediments occur. Many obstacles were invented to create delay. A memorandum has been handed to Government, annexed to the copy of plan of Mocha, which contains the remarks made during my stay at that place.

tempted to recross the desert to the Persian Gulf, many had died of fatigue; the few who arrived were stripped of everything they possessed, even to their shirts, and were treated in the most barbarous manner by the Bedouins. My Moonshee was one of the few who arrived; he had been plundered of every thing he possessed, letters, papers, &c. The Bedouins whom I despatched from Rus had never delivered their letters; as only a part of the reward for conveying them had been paid, and the remaining sum, which was the more considerable, was made payable on delivery at Kutteef, and of which they were perfectly confident, I am inclined to think that they were plundered by the Bedouins of the other tribes, through whose camps they must have passed.

The papers of which the Moonshee had been deprived were by me considered as very interesting. They contained the names of all the places through which we had passed, written correctly in the Arabic character, and also the names of the tribes, with their divisions, or more properly a catalogue of the smaller tribes and families of which the principal ones are composed, together with some remarks respecting them. This man was a native of Aboosheere, of the Sheeah faith; after performing the Zeearut at Medina, he set off direct for Mecca, under a promise of rejoining me at Yambo when he had become a Hajee, to which I freely consented. On arriving at Mecca he joined the Hajees of his own persuasion, and they generally remain ten days after the Soonees to perform their devotions without interruption, to which they are very liable, as the Turks retain nearly the same antipathy to a Rafuzee as to a Christian. The Meerza unfortunately listened to the advice of a Persian Khan, who had made a tour through Egypt, and had been the bearer of letters and presents to Muhmud Ali Pacha from the King of Persia, requesting the protection of Muhmud Ali, in favour of the Persian Sheeah pilgrims; he accompanied this Khan to Medina, where the great man departed this life; and thence set out on his way to recross the desert to the Persian Gulf, in company with the caravan of pilgrims, which paid a large sum to Ibrahim for protecting them to Heeneekah, the frontier post of the Turks, who would not venture beyond this limit for any reward that could be offered. The Turks returned immediately to Medina, leaving the Bussorah and Persian pilgrims to the mercy of the Bedouins, who commenced to exact money and plunder them. As they could not make good their return to Medina they had now no other alternative than to submit. Muhmud Ali Pacha has contrived to make himself a person of great consequence in the Mahomedan world, since the period of his having become the protector of the holy land of Mahomed. He receives every year the most flattering letters, accompanied with rich presents sent by different Mahomedan princes, even from India, and the most distant parts. His Majesty the King of Persia has sent several letters prior to that alluded to this year, with a view to gain the good graces of the Pacha, and through his influence to obtain permission for some persons to visit Medina in his name, and there to offer up prayers, and make offerings at the shrine of the prophet; but in this object I can assure His Majesty he will never succeed. As I entertain sentiments of the highest respect for the king of kings, I would recommend him to effect his salvation through the medium of Ali, at whose shrine his diamonds, emeralds, rubies, and feeroozas, will be eagerly accepted, and through whose intercession he has equally as good a chance of inducing the divine providence to defer the visit of Asrail, of whose approach it would be treason to offer the most distant hint to His Majesty. I fear if this pious king should ever fall into the hands of Mahomed Ali, he would discover too late, that the Pacha has been one of that angel's most active and expert vicegerents.

APPENDICES.

INSTRUCTIONS.

SECRET DEPARTMENT.

To Captain G. F. SADLEIR, &c. &c. &c.

SIR,—The Right Honourable the Governor in Council having deemed it necessary that an officer should be entrusted with the charge of a confidential despatch from His Excellency the Most Noble the Governor General to His Excellency Ibrahim Pacha (son of the Pacha of Egypt) now in the command of the Turkish army employed in Arabia against the Wahabee power inhabiting the western coasts of the Gulf of Persia, and to concert the necessary arrangements with His Excellency with a view to the complete reduction of that power, I have the honour of acquainting you that, having the most perfect reliance in your prudence and discretion, he has been pleased to confide the execution of this important service to you.

2. You are already apprized that His Excellency Ibrahim Pacha had the good fortune, a few months since, to obtain possession of Deriah, and to seize the person of Sooltan bin Saood,* the chieftain of the Wahabees, and that His Excellency has followed up his successes to the shores of the Persian Gulf, intending, as it is understood, to retaliate on the piratical tribes for the cruelties they have committed on the subjects of the Sublime Porte, to whom unfortunately those cruelties have not been confined, but have been extended to other states on this side of India. In effecting this object the Governor General is willing to afford His Excellency the aid of the British Government, and is therefore desirous that a communication should be had with Ibrahim Pacha for the purpose of learning from His Excellency in what manner the naval and military forces at our command

---

* Abdoolah bin Saood.

can be best applied in conjunction with the Turkish army, in facilitating His Excellency's operations in the reduction of the Joassimees, and for inflicting on them that punishment with which crimes of such unparalleled atrocity require to be visited.

3. You will therefore be pleased to embark on board the Honorable Company's Cruiser "Thetis," whose Commander has been instructed, as per accompanying copy of my letter to the Superintendent of Marine of the 7th instant, to receive you and convey you to one of the ports in the Persian Gulf in the possession of the Turkish forces, which, according to the intelligence you may be able to obtain at Muscat, may appear to be most convenient to enable you to effect a speedy communication with Ibrahim Pacha, and on meeting His Excellency, you will deliver to him the letter above mentioned, with the sword intended for His Excellency, as also a letter from the Right Honorable the Governor of this Presidency, bearing His Excellency's address; copies of which, both in the English and Native versions, are now transmitted to you for your information.

4. If, as most probably will be the case, His Excellency Ibrahim Pacha should be desirous of availing himself of the aid of the British Government, he will of course communicate freely with you on the plans he may have in contemplation, and you are authorized to assure His Excellency that as soon after the termination of the monsoon as may be favourable for undertaking operations from hence, we shall be prepared to send an adequate naval and military force to the Gulf of Persia, for the purpose of cöoperating with His Excellency in the reduction of Rus-ul-Khima, which will afterwards be delivered over to be garrisoned by the Turkish troops, provided His Excellency shall allot a competent force to the service of covering the siege.

5. But whatever His Excellency's plans may be with a view to further conquest, it will not be necessary that you should pledge the British Government to secure to His Excellency the possession of any such conquests without receiving further instructions from Government.

6. During your stay with His Excellency you will endeavour to ascertain the extent and description of the force under His Excellency's command, and the extent and nature of the assistance he may expect to derive from the British Government.

7. As it will be necessary that you should touch at Muscat on your way to the Gulf, you will, on landing at that place, solicit an interview of the Imam, and make known to him the nature of the communication which you are authorized to open with Ibrahim Pacha; you will likewise ascertain from His Highness the nature and extent of the assistance he may be able to afford in the reduction of the piratical ports.

8. The Governor in Council directs me to transmit for your information a copy of a letter written by him to His Highness the Imam, the original of which will also be delivered to you before your departure, informing him of the service confided to you, together with a copy of his letter to His Highness, of the 15th January, as also an extract of a letter from Captain Taylor at Muscat, dated the 29th of that month.

9. During your residence in the Turkish camp, you will endeavour to ascertain, with as much delicacy as possible, the nature of Ibrahim Pacha's views in the further prosecution of his conquests on the Arabian shores of the Persian Gulf, without showing any material interest on the subject.

10. You will also collect every possible information regarding the nature and resources of the country, the number and extent of the towns in the interior, and on any points which may appear to you to be interesting as connected with a country so little known.

11. Having arranged all your plans, and received from His Excellency such communications as he may have to convey to His Excellency the Governor General or to the Governor of this Presidency, you will return to this place; first explaining to the officer in command of His Majesty's and the Honorable Company's ships employed in the Gulf, the plans you may have concerted, that he may regulate his conduct in the promotion of the measures which may have been decided upon for the attainment of the objects we have mutually in view.

12. Whilst employed on this duty the Governor in Council is pleased to allow you to draw a personal salary of Rupees 800 per mensem from the 1st instant, and to charge on honor for your expenses, which you will be careful to confine within as narrow limits as possible.

13. The Residents at Bushire and Bussora have been advised of your mission to the Turkish Camp, and directed to afford you any assistance which you may require; you will likewise draw on those officers, as you may find to be most practicable and convenient, for the requisite funds to meet your disbursements.

14. You have been furnished with a stock of presents, for delivery to such of the Turkish officers as may meet you in your route, and who may assist you in your progress to and from the Turkish camp. You will keep a regular return, showing to whom these presents have been issued, and such as you may not find occasion to distribute, are to be delivered into store on your return to Bombay.

15. You will receive herewith a despatch for His Majesty's Consul General in Egypt, advising him of your mission to the Turkish Camp, and enclosing copies of the letters addressed to His Excellency by the Governor General and the Governor of Bombay, which you will take an opportunity of forwarding to Mr. Salt by any of His Excellency's messengers that may be proceeding to Egypt, accompanied by a letter from yourself, explaining the nature of your reception, and the period of your stay with His Excellency.

I have the honour to be, &c.,

(Signed) WM. NEWNHAM,

Acting Chief Secretary.

Bombay Castle, 13th April 1819.

Copy.

To Ibrahim Pacha.
Written 2nd January 1819.

I have been gratified by the information recently transmitted to me of the brilliant success of the arms of the Ottoman Empire, under the personal direction of your Excellency. The particulars of the capture of Deriah having been communicated to me, I eagerly seize the occasion of congratulating you on the ardent bravery and distinguished judgment and conduct by which the march of your army has been so early and so honorably signalized, and of which the proud result has been the entire defeat and downfall of a power, which, after an extraordinary and rapid rise to very considerable eminence, it was happily reserved for your Excellency finally to humble. The ground of offering my congratulations and the pledge of their sincerity, are to be found in the circumstance of my having had the good fortune to be engaged in much friendly correspondence with your respected father, Mohammed Ali Pacha, the Viceroy of Egypt; the sentiments of respect and regard which I entertain for His Highness, and which his unvarying friendship and good will towards the British Government are so well calculated to foster and strengthen, must ever lead me to rejoice in the prosperous issue of exertions made under his auspices. But my gratification is, I assure you, much augmented by having congratulations to make on an occasion on which the glory of his son and the successes of his arms have become inseparably connected.

It has been reported to me that your Excellency now purposes to employ your victorious troops in reducing to obedience the other refractory chiefs, and principally the Joassimees. It has probably come to your knowledge that the daring piracies and outrages committed by the last mentioned tribe in the Persian Gulf, and the cruelties which have been exercised by their crews, have also placed them in the condition of enemies to the British Government. We have thence been led to contemplate measures for their early chastisement, and I have reflected on the probability of the object of your Excellency's policy, and of our intended proceedings being expediently attained by a combination of the efforts of the two Governments. A joint cöoperation between the army which your Excellency commands, and a military and naval force to be furnished by the British Government, appears to me to be a most advantageous and desirable course. Should your Excellency's judgment be inclined to approve this measure, I beg to refer you to the Right Honorable Sir Evan Nepean, the Governor of Bombay, to whom my sentiments on this point are entirely known, and whose communications respecting the mode of cöoperation, and the period at which it can conveniently be carried into effect, I solicit you to regard in the same manner as if they came directly from myself. Should the design which I have had the honour to suggest to your Excellency's considerations be adopted, the details of the arrangement will be most expeditiously and suitably concerted beween your Excellency or your officers acting under sufficient powers, and gentlemen on the part of the British Government furnished with ample authority and instructions from the Right Honorable the Governor of Bombay.

As a slight token of personal esteem and consideration I entreat your acceptance of a sword, which will be transmitted from Calcutta, with this letter, and will be forwarded to you by the Governor of Bombay.

Believe, &c.

(A true copy)

  (Signed)   J. ADAM,
     Chief Secretary to Government.

(True copy)

  (Signed)   W. NEWNHAM,
     Acting Chief Secretary.

To His Excellency IBRAHIM PACHA.

Although I have not hitherto had the honour of a direct correspondence with your Excellency, and personally unknown to you, I cannot refrain from taking advantage of the opportunity afforded to me by the transmission of a letter to your Excellency from the Most Noble the Governor General, of offering you my warmest congratulations on the brilliant successes with which the promptitude and energy of your measures for the destruction of the Wahabee power, and the valour of your troops, have been attended, which cannot fail to attract the notice of your august Sovereign, and to secure to your Excellency the admiration and applause of your respected father, with whom I have been in habits of cordial correspondence.

The splendid advantages gained by your Excellency, and the rapid advance of your army to the shores of the Persian Gulf, have led me to anticipate that your Excellency will follow up your successes for the suppression of the power of the Joassimees, who have so long infested the Gulf, and have even extended their piratical operations to the coasts of Arabia and Mekran, in which they have been but too successful.

It cannot have escaped your Excellency's knowledge, that the unparalleled atrocities of the Joassimees, and other piratical tribes in connection with them, have determined the British Government to have recourse to such measures as may be most effectual for inflicting upon them that chastisement which their cruelties so justly deserve.

The naval and military force destined for this service will proceed to the Gulf of Persia as soon after the close of the monsoon as the season may be favorable for that purpose, and under an impression that your Excellency may be desirous of availing yourself of the proximity of this force to act in concert with it, I have determined to depute Captain Sadleir, an officer who possesses my entire confidence, to your Excellency's camp for the purpose of communicating with your Excellency on this important subject. That officer will deliver to your Excellency the letter from His Excellency the Most Noble the Governor General to which I have alluded, and will, I am persuaded, feel no difficulty in satisfying your Excellency of the friendly disposition of the British Government, and in concerting with you such a plan of combined operations as will ensure the most complete attainment of the objects now in comtemplation.

Having thus communicated to your Excellency the general view of the British Government, I trust your Excellency will permit me to refer you to Captain Sadlier for particulars, and that you will accept the assurances of regard and esteem with which

I have the honour to be, &c. &c.,

(Signed) EVAN NEPEAN.

Bombay Castle, 5th April 1819.

(True copy)
(Signed) WM. NEWNHAM,
Acting Chief Secretary.

Copy of a letter from the Right Honorable Sir EVAN NEPEAN, *Bart., Governor of Bombay, to the* IMAM *of* MUSKAT, *dated the 12th April* 1819.

I have the pleasure of acknowledging your Highness' obliging letter of the 3rd of Rubeessance in reply to the one I entrusted to Captain Taylor for delivery to your Highness, and I am happy that the information communicated in it, regarding the measures to be adopted by this Government for the destruction of the piratical powers in the Gulf, proved satisfactory to your Highness.

I now take the liberty of introducing to your Highness Captain Sadlier, who is charged with a commission to his Excellency Ibrahim Pacha, the object of which is to concert with

His Excellency the plan of a joint co-operation against Rus-ul-Khima. That officer is completely in the confidence of Government, and will be ready to communicate with your Highness on any points connected with that object.

(A true copy)

(Signed)   R. T. GOODWIN,
Secretary and Translator in the Office of
Country Correspondence.

(A true copy)

(Signed)   WILLIAM NEWNHAM,
Acting Chief Secretary to Government.

A.

To the Right Honourable Sir E. Nepean, Bart.,
　　　　　　　　President and Governor in Council.

Right Honourable Sir,

I have the honour to acquaint you that after a most tedious passage of twenty-four days the Honorable Company's Cruiser "Thetis" anchored in the cove of Muscat on the evening of 7th May. H. M.'s Ship "Curlew," commanded by Captain Walpole, which sailed from Bombay ten days subsequent to our departure, arrived here early on the following morning, and I had the honour to pay my first visit to His Highness the Imam, accompanied by Captain Walpole and Lieutenant Tanner, when your letter to His Highness's address was presented by me. His Highness received the communication with apparent satisfaction, and expressed the high sense he entertains of the friendly alliance and good understanding which has uniformly existed between the Honorable Company's Government and his family, and from which he has received such constant support. As it was necessary to afford His Highness leisure to peruse your letter, our conversation was of course directed to other topics; indeed His Highness's Minister Sheikh Ali-bin-Fazel, who was the person deputed by the Imam to receive me, and arrange the interview, stated that he had been directed to intimate to me the wishes of the Imam on this particular occasion. The Minister and His Highness's brother, Seyud Salim, were the only persons present on the part of the Imam, who introduced each of them in their respective situations.

His Highness communicated to Captain Walpole the information received at Muscat of the return of twelve Joassmee vessels, which had been traced as far as Bab-ul-Mandul. It appears that of the seventeen vessels which sailed from Ras-ul-Khima, twelve have been spoken with off Fuzeerah, a small harbour situated between Khor-Chelha and Khor-Fekhan, a place lately taken possession of by the Joassmee pirates, and where these twelve boats had touched about four days ago to obtain information. Their cruise has been attended with very little advantage, as they are reported to have captured only two small boats belonging to Socrota, and the value of which must be very trifling.

This information induced Captain Walpole to determine on joining the Imam's vessels cruising off Cape Mussendom, and His Highness having addressed letters to the Commanders of those vessels, the "Curlew" put to sea on the evening of the 8th instant.

His Highness's Minister called on me on the evening of 8th, and entered into a long discussion on the subject of the intended expedition, which I soon discovered was introduced as a prelude to inquiries which he had been directed to make as to the purpose of my mission to the Turkish camp, and although he endeavoured to conceal both his anxiety and curiosity, it was evident that his mind, or possibly his master's mind, was not altogether at rest on this point. I assured him that the British Government was extremely anxious to witness a good understanding between the Turkish general and His Highness the Imam; that the friendly intercourse which has subsisted between His Highness Mahomed Ali Pacha and the British Government may be considered as the best security for the foundation of the friendship, which I trusted would be more closely cemented between the Imam and His Excellency Ibrahim Pacha, whose exertions and perseverance in exterminating the Wahabees have justly entitled him to our praise; and the success which has hitherto attended the arms of Ibrahim Pacha must, no doubt, have materially affected the political state of this country, and conduced to the safety and tranquillity of His Highness the Imam's dominions, as well as to the advancement of the general happiness and security of the neighbouring states. That His Excellency Ibrahim Pacha was of course aware of the friendly relations existing between the British Government and His Highness the Imam; therefore on that head it was unnecessary to enter into a discussion on points which in all reasonable expectation never could arise. I requested him to convey to the Imam these my sentiments and opinions on this subject, and to solicit an interview on the following day, which he promised to effect.

On the morning of the 9th the Minister again called on me, and again agitated the subject introduced yesterday. I offered every argument that could possibly tend to convince him how unnecessary such surmises must eventually prove. He then communicated the intelligence he had received on the evening of 8th, subsequent to his visit to me, that the Fort of Brimee (situated in the interior, about two days' march from Rus-ul-Khima, and an equal distance from Shargeh) had been surrendered to an officer of the Imam's, who had been deputed to offer conditions and terms to Buttal Wahabee. This chief had been induced to withdraw from the interests of his former associates, who were inclined to effect his removal, and possibly his death. Under these circumstances he conceived it prudent to effect a reconciliation with the Imam, who has promised him protection, and finding himself pressed on the one hand by Sultan-bin Suggar and Rushud-bin-Humeed, who were originally joined in league with the Rus-ul-Khima Joassmees, but at the present moment, as the Minister states, separated in their interests. Buttal followed the more prudent measure of surrendering to the Imam, and the chiefs of the district of Brimee have sworn allegiance to the Imam, whose officers now retain possession of the place; Sultan-bin-Suggar of Shargeh and his associate Rushud-bin-Humeed of Ajmaan, wish to induce the Imam to deliver over Brimee to Suggar, who says he will retain it for the Imam, with whom they are at present inclined to court an apparent friendship. I offered some remarks on the danger of His Highness being deluded by false appearances, and recommended the Minister to be cautious in advising a temporary reconciliation by which those enemies to society may screen themselves at the moment they expect to be visited with the punishment they deserve.

I proposed to accompany the Minister agreeably to the arrangement of yesterday, but he excused himself for the present, and said it would be better to defer till evening our visit to the Imam, who was at present sitting in public, where such matters could not be fitly discussed; that the Imam expected the arrival of the Brimee chief on the morning of the 10th; would wish to defer till then our second interview. To this proposal I objected, as I wished to convey to His Highness the expectations entertained by the British Government of his cordial support in the ensuing expedition, which formed the subject of my mission to Muscat, but that I of course would attend on the morning of the 10th. The Minister promised to arrange an interview in the evening, but on his arrival, about five o'clock, I found him inclined to enter upon some other topics not at all connected with the object of my visit to Muscat, and that he was still inclined to defer to some distant period the explanation which I required. I therefore urged the necessity of adhering to the promise made in the forenoon, on which he departed, and I was shortly after summoned to attend the Imam. The subject of the conference I shall minutely detail.

On the evening of the 9th I obtained an interview with His Highness, on which occasion he was attended by his Minister Sheikh Alie-bin-Fazell, and Goolah Anandass, the accredited Broker of the Honorable Company, was present. His Highness shortly after my arrival remarked that in the letter which I had presented to him, he observed that it was intended I should proceed to Deriah to the camp of His Excellency Ibrahim Pacha, to concert with that General; also on the intended expedition; to which I replied in the affirmative. His Highness said that he had occasion to write to Ibrahim Pacha respecting Bahrein, but that as he had not received an answer he presumed that it was necessary in all cases to await a reply from or reference to His Highness Muhumud Alie Pacha, as Ibrahim Pacha could not act in those matters without orders; that the delay would certainly exceed the period fixed for the sailing of the expedition, and he wished to know whether the expedition would be deferred till my return, which even from Deriah could not possibly be expected, as he surmised, previous to the period alluded to. I replied that no delay whatever should be imputed to me, as I should exert my utmost diligence; that if Ibrahim Pacha coincided in our views, I conceived it would be unnecessary to refer to Muhumud Alie Pacha; that I entertained little doubt on these two points, and that the expedition, as has been stated to him, is now in preparation, therefore would of course be in readiness to proceed; however, that it was not at all likely that my not returning would interfere in the arrangements. His Highness repeatedly endeavoured to impress on my mind the impossibility of accomplishing my journey in time to convey an answer; after which he inquired of me if I had heard of the conduct of Ibrahim Pacha toward the Arabs at Deriah, or elsewhere, intimating that cruelties had been committed by that General. Of this accusation I declared my ignorance, and His Highness replied that on my arrival there I would be better informed. I used every argument to remove from the mind of the Imam any unfavorable impression he may entertain of Ibrahim Pacha, by drawing his attention to the conduct of Muhumud Alie Pacha in Egypt, and to the good understanding existing between the British Government and His Highness, and repeated all the arguments that I had adduced in the two conferences with his Minister on this subject. He asked me if it was possible to effect the object without the interference of strangers, or without calling for the assistance of the Turkish army. I replied that if it were possible I should be happy to pay attention and deference to his opinions if he would do me the favour to communicate them, and that I should even convey them to my Government; but however I conceived it my duty to draw his attention to the communication he had made to Captain Taylor. It may appear inconsistent that at one period he should have proposed to offer his own vessels in aid of the Pacha's views, and now entertain any difficulty as to the policy of joining us in conjunction with the Turkish army, as this proposal from himself was the most particular inducement to expect his most cordial assistance, particularly as he had led Captain Taylor to suppose that he did not labour under any apprehension from the views of the Pacha towards himself.

I therefore trusted that his mind was perfectly at rest on this point, and concluded with these remarks, which had been communicated in the morning to his Minister.

The expedition contemplated at the present crisis is intended to consist of nearly four times the number of troops, and of a much more formidable naval equipment than that which His Highness had the pleasure to witness on a former occasion, therefore the assistance to be afforded us in the completion of our view must of course be on an equally enlarged and extensive scale; the benefits resulting from such combined efforts on so efficient and general a plan must be self-evident, and it is probable that His Highness will gain more direct advantage from these effects than any chief or power concerned.

His Highness must be perfectly aware that the British Government does not contemplate either increase of territory or revenues by the subjection of the Wahabees or the Joassmee pirates; our Government is stimulated most particularly by a desire to avenge the insults and injuries offered to the peaceable inhabitants of neighbouring states in terms of amity with us, from the connection with whom by trade and intercourse, our subjects certainly derive mercantile influence and profit; as far as relates individually to ourselves we have it in our power to protect our own trade by our ships of war; our policy is not limited to our own private view, and we expect that all powers in amity with us, whose locality enables them to afford assistance, will come forward, and enter in the subjugation of the pirate tribes, affording every possible assistance.

The letter addressed to His Highness and delivered to him by Captain Taylor most fully explains the feelings which actuate the British Government with respect to our intentions towards himself, and of our sincere desire to witness a friendly understanding between His Highness and Ibrahim Pacha.

I next brought to his recollection the benefits which had resulted from Ibrahim Pacha's perseverance in the war against the Wahabees, and the policy of availing ourselves of his proximity to completely effect the purpose proposed. I brought forward an argument adduced by His Highness himself, as to the possibility of the Turkish army being removed, and argued the bad policy of procrastination. After some consideration His Highness distinctly replied to me that he had long since determined on one point, to whch he should strictly adhere; for although he acknowledged the truth of many of my arguments, he had determined not to allow his troops to associate on shore in concert with the Turkish army, as the consequences may be fatal to him; and further that he could not compel his troops to obey such orders; but that he would give a general assurance of support and assistance whenever the expedition should arrive; that he would accompany the expedition himself, and embark five thousand troops to act in concert and associate with the British, effecting any purpose in conjunction with our troops which the capacity of his army would admit of; but that it must be expressly understood that if the Turkish army acted in the interior he could not be called upon to associate his troops with them; that if the Turkish army should not be called upon he would endeavour to procure a sufficient force to act in the interior; also that at the present moment he could not enter into particulars, but would defer till to-morrow the future deliberations; however, that His Highness's objection to associate with Ibrahim Pacha's army on shore precluded him from committing to writing any part of those assurances; and in reply to a question which I urged with delicacy, but with reference to the capture of Ras-ul-Khima on the former occasion, His Highness declared his incapacity to retain it, if it was even offered to him, alleging the expense attendant on this measure as an insurmountable barrier. His Highness having expressed his acknowledgment of the delicacy observed on my part in offering my opinions and arguments to his consideration, I withdrew, on his appointing the following day for a second conference.

On the morning of the 10th I had the pleasure to receive a communication from the Minister, that His Highness had fully reconsidered the remarks which I had the pleasure to offer for his consideration on the foregoing evening, and that at or before eleven he would be happy to accompany me to the presence of the Imam.

I accordingly met the Minister, and after some general remarks he said that all difficulties would be easily removed; we therefore proceeded to the Imam's Palace. We found His Highness and his brother seated with him. After a little hesitation the Imam said he would enter into any particulars that were considered necessary. We therefore entered upon the state of the Joassmees as they now exist.

His Highness represented their power to be on the decline since the overthrow of the Wahabee chief, and which has given rise to the want of confidence in the different chiefs towards each other, or rather the conviction of the determination of each to advance his own interests at the expense of his neighbour's. This state of things he conceives to be very favourable; the want of a leader of talents and the present confined and cramped state of the Joassmees since the overthrow of the Wahabees may probably breed dissension among them. Very few of those who escaped from Deriah have joined the Joassmees; he does not estimate the number at more than three hundred. The following estimate of the whole force of the Joassmees, as they now exist, he had collected from the very best authority, and considers it as authentic:—

```
                                                         Foot.
Joined from the remains of the Wahabee force say      300
 1. Bukha, contains only .............................  20
 2. Shaam .....................................150 to 200
 3. Rums ..............................................200
 4. Ras-ul-Khima, large boats 25, small 75, and     3,000
 5. Humrah, all joined at Ras-ul-Khima.
 6. Oomul Goweyn, large boats 1  small 30  ......   400
 7. Ajmaan                   „    4  „  35  ......1,000
 8. Fusht, with    ⎫
 9. Shargeh, and   ⎬  „  12  „  150  ......1,280
10. Aboo Heyle     ⎭
11. Dubyee                „    4  „  100  ......  800
                           „  46  „  390  ......7,200
```

Boo Dubyee (Khyram Bineeyas), large 5, small 300, 3,000 foot.

This last port can scarcely be considered as a pirate port, having been long disunited from Ras-ul-Khima.

To the east of Cape Mussendom is the small bay of Fugeerah, which serves as a look-out port on this side for boats coming up the Gulf. As before remarked in the 2nd paragraph of this letter, from Fugeerah or from Dubah an Arab Causid can pass the mountains to Rus-ul-Khima in fourteen hours; the road from Dubah is passable for foot and horse, and even for small guns, and the journey can be effected in two days.

The present disposition of the Shargeh chief may probably induce him, as well as the chief of Ajmaan, to remain disunited from the chief of Rus-ul-Khima pending the hostilities. His Highness has therefore declared his intention to use his endeavours to effect this object, although he recommends the whole to meet with the same fate that may attend Rus-ul-Khima.

I then proposed to His Highness that we should take into consideration the measures to be adopted in the offensive operations. After some circumlocution and argument, His Highness agreed to the following arrangements, which he requested me to commit to writing, and to transmit to your Honourable Board, in reply to that part of my instructions touching the nature and extent of the assistance he may be able to afford in the reduction of the piratical port.

With a view to preventing the fugitive Joassmees of Rus-ul-Khima from entering into Oman, His Highness intends to post a sufficient number of men in the passes of the mountains, pending the operations against Rus-ul-Khima, should the services of those men not be required in consequence of the arrival of the Pacha's army; but if that event does not take place His Highness will be prepared to co-operate by land with a force of seven thousand foot, one hundred and thirty cavalry, and fifteen hundred camels, to proceed by the passes above Rus-ul-Khima, and invest that place; he himself will accompany the expedition in a ship of war, and take with him at least one thousand men to be landed and to act in conjunction with the British force, it being understood, that if Ibrahim Pacha's force acts by land the Imam's force will all proceed by sea, except that part required for the purpose already stated of guarding the passes into Oman; the necessary precautions will of course be taken to prevent the Arab and Turkish soldiery being employed in conjunction with each other, and their camps shall be at all times separate.

The next assistance to be afforded on his part appeared to be the supply of boats to assist in the disembarkation of troops, baggage, &c. Unfortunately the number of the description required for that purpose is much diminished within these few years. His Highness stated that he could not promise a greater number than seventy, but if possible he would increase the number to one hundred, each capable of conveying from thirty to fifty men.

With respect to water and firewood His Highness stated that a sufficiency of each should be supplied at His Highness's expense, but that cattle and such other supplies as were necessary would be procured more readily by our own Commissary, who would pay only the regulated price, His Highness exerting his influence to prevent over-charge.

His Highness consents to employ two of his ships for the conveyance of stores, or in whatever way they may be best applied, agreeable to the wishes of the British Government, at whose disposal two ships will be placed, whenever the Right Honourable the Governor in Council may intimate his wishes on that subject to His Highness.

His Highness will continue to keep up a correspondence with the Government of Bombay on all subjects connected with the advancement of the preparations for the expedition, and will forward every information that he may obtain relative to any alterations that may take place in the force or numbers of the Joassmee pirates, so that the Government may at all times be perfectly acquainted with the actual state of their power.

His Highness concluded with a general assurance of support and assistance, and stated that any measures adopted by the British

Government should meet with his warmest support; that independent of the particulars here enumerated, he would be happy to forward the views of Government by attending to any arrangements that might have been omitted in the foregoing outline.

I have every reason to imagine that His Highness will use his best efforts to complete the arrangements so as to enable him to fulfil the engagements and assurances which I have now the honor to transmit to your Honourable Board, and I trust I shall not be deemed presumptuous in offering my opinion on the motives which I imagine induced the Imam to hesitate at the first interview. It is very obvious that the introduction of Ibrahim Pacha's force and the proximity of the scene of action to the boundary of His Highness's territory, are two subjects which give rise to feelings of jealousy and suspicion in the mind of the Imam, particularly when it is recollected that the Pacha's views towards obtaining possession of Bahrein have become public, and that he has not satisfied the Imam's inquiries on that subject. The Imam therefore in the first instance appears to have had in view the possibility of inducing me to give up the idea of proceeding to Deriah, first arguing the distance and delay, next the possibility of effecting the overthrow of the Joassmees without the assistance of the Pacha. Not having carried this point, he next assayed to obtain a pledge from me on the part of the British Government. To this I invariably replied by repeating that part of the letter addressed by the Right Honourable the Governor in Council to His Highness, and on no occasion did I exceed the limits of the assurances conveyed in that address.

As it is probable I shall touch at Muscat on my return to Bombay at a period when it will be necessary to observe whether these preparations are in a state of forwardness, I trust I shall then be favored with directions for the guidance of my conduct under the following circumstances. First, should Ibrahim Pacha decline to move any part of his army to so great a distance from Deriah or Lahissa, what further assistance to the accomplishment of the views of the British Government would be required on the part of the Imam of Muscat? Secondly, should Ibrahim Pacha accept the proposals offered to him, what assurances may I feel myself at liberty to make to the Imam of Muscat in order to set his mind at rest, and to suppress the doubts which he appears to entertain of the Pacha's views?

From the information I have collected here from other sources I do not imagine that the Imam has underrated the forces of the Joassmees, neither can I learn from any authority on which I could depend, that the Arabs of the interior will come forward to assist the Joassmees of Rus-ul Khima; if they were inclined to join their former associates the number of men they could bring into the field would not exceed three thousand, and if the Brimee chief and his associates can be depended upon, even that number would be considerably diminished. It appears that the Imam's force amounts to twenty thousand foot-men, distributed throughout the villages and along the coast; but although every Arab is a soldier and armed, it is not to be supposed that the army is disposable; of the twenty thousand foot it is probable ten thousand may be collected at one point, and of his cavalry not more than one hundred and thirty, or one hundred and fifty.

I shall not presume to offer an opinion on the qualifications of His Highness's army, as they have been already brought to the notice of your Honourable Board by officers who have had a better opportunity of forming an opinion on that subject, during the former expedition.

I have been this day honoured by the receipt of His Highness's amended letter, in which he has been pleased to authenticate the assurances and promises of assistance communicated by His Highness's desire in this despatch, and I trust that the Right Honourable the Governor in Council (to whose address His Highness's despatch is addressed, in reply to that with which I had the honour to be entrusted) will be pleased to approve of the result of my endeavours to promote the views of Government.

I have the honour to acquaint you that I have availed myself of the very able advice and extensive information communicated to me by Captain Lock, R. N. I have in consequence determined to proceed in the first instance to Bushire, with a view to obtaining correct information respecting the harbour of Kutteef, and the route to Deriah, where I hope I may have the good fortune to find His Excellency Ibrahim Pacha's camp situated. The reports in circulation here do not promise an easy access to Deriah, but of this I shall be able to speak with more certainty after my arrival at Bushire.

I have the honour to be, &c.

Muscat, 15th May 1819.

B.

To the Honourable M. ELPHINSTONE,

    Governor and President in Council, Bombay.

HONOURABLE SIR,

I have the honour to acquaint your Honourable Board, that my intention of returning to Bussorah having been frustrated, as mentioned in my letter of 26th August, I was under the necessity of proceeding towards Medina, in the neighbourhood of which city I was met by His Excellency's Peshkur Aghasee, who had received instructions to conduct me to Bir Alee, situated three miles on the other side the city. The circuitous route which this guide selected, to preclude the possibility of my beholding this seat of Mahomedan superstition and fanaticism, protracted our arrival till night, when I was indebted to His Excellency's Physician, an Italian gentleman, for the hospitality of my reception.

His Excellency visited Bir Alee the following evening (8th September) at a late hour, and as he was not provided with any accommodation for public reception he alighted at the tent of the gentleman to whom I have before alluded, and deputed him to request I would pay him a visit, at which ceremony would be dispensed with, and public business would not be introduced. I attended His Excellency, who received me courteously, and on his offering an apology for the length and fatigues of the journey I had been obliged to endure, I expressed my regret that I had not had the good fortune to reach His Excellency's camp when at Deriah, which would have afforded me the satisfaction of offering the congratulations of the British authorities in India, by whom I had been deputed to His Excellency, on the spot which had been the scene of His Excellency's victories and successes. To this His Excellency replied that unforeseen events and disappointments had precluded the possibility of my joining him at an earlier period, and that his departure from Rus was occasioned by very urgent business at Medina; that my return from

Rus to Bussorah would not have met with his approbation, as the route was unsafe, and he could not have detached an escort.

His Excellency's inquiries were then directed to India and the British Government established there, of which he appeared to possess a very superficial knowledge. After a conversation, which was protracted till midnight, His Excellency expressed a wish to confer with me on the subject of the communications I was entrusted with, and appointed the following morning. As my tents were conveniently situated, His Excellency proposed that the interview should take place there. He then retired to his harem, which was encamped at Bir Alee.

On the morning of the 9th I had the honour to receive His Excellency, and to present to him the despatches of the Most Noble the Governor General, and the Right Honorable the Governor in Council of Bombay, both of which His Excellency appeared to peruse. His Excellency, addressing himself to me, remarked, that heretofore he had not been honored with any direct communication from the Government of India, and had only been known to that Government through the medium of the friendly correspondence which had existed between his father and the British authorities in India. To which I replied, that the present communication was the foundation of a personal and permanent friendship, which I trusted would be continued without any interruption. I then presented to His Excellency the sword which had been entrusted to my charge. His Excellency appeared highly gratified by the congratulations offered, and the favor which accompanied them.

After a short complimentary conversation, His Excellency directed the attendants to withdraw, and again perused the despatches which I had the honour to present. During the confidential communication which ensued, His Excellency informed me that the policy of this expedition had been entrusted to his father's guidance by the Ottoman Court. His Excellency's instructions had limited his operations to Deriah, but that he was not aware of the ultimate views which had actuated that court to set on foot the expedition. On the fall of Deriah His Excellency awaited further instructions, which arrived from Constantinople, directing the total destruction of Deriah, and eventually the evacuation of the whole country, the revenues of which were reported insufficient to defray the expenses of the troops required for its protection during His Excellency's stay at Deriah. Awaiting these orders he had pushed a post as far as Ul-Ahsa and Kateef, to procure supplies, his army being in the greatest distress, and that at that period a friendly intercourse with the British would have proved of the first importance.

His Excellency expressed his regret at the altered state of affairs, which would preclude the possibility of his meeting the wishes of the Most Noble the Governor General, in whose views he would have been most happy to have coincided at an earlier period, had he been acquainted with the intentions of the British authorities; he however considered the communication to be of such importance as to require a reference to His Highness the Viceroy, without whose instructions he was averse to form a reply to the despatches.

My anxiety to prevent a further detention, induced me to express a hope that His Excellency would reconsider the subject, and if possible, avoid the delay which must ensue in awaiting an answer from Cairo. His Excellency would not however acquiesce in my solicitations, and I found myself obliged to consent to his referring a subject to Cairo, which had been most fully elucidated ere I had the misfortune to enter the province of Nedjed.

His Excellency requested me to address a letter to Mr. Salt explanatory of the communications I had made to him, and to transmit it as an accompaniment to the despatches which he should forward to His Highness Muhumud Ali Pacha, who may refer to or consult with Mr. Salt, if necessary. I therefore transmitted the letter of the Chief Secretary of Government to Mr. Salt's address, and laid before him the particulars of the conference, with a request to use his influence to expedite my departure for India.

As the port of Jeddah promised the most probable chance of procuring a passage to Mocha, I requested His Excellency to permit me to accompany him on the route towards Mecca, and thence to Jeddah, there to await his return from the pilgrimage;

to which he at first accorded, but ultimately altered my destination for Yambo on the plea of the inconvenience which would arise from detaching a few horsemen for the two stages from the point where these roads separate. His Excellency mentioned his determination of returning *viâ* Yambo, where he purposed to afford me the honor of another interview, and there arrange his reply. I was therefore obliged to proceed with the escort which protected His Excellency's harem to Yambo, from whence they were to be embarked for Suez. My stay at this miserable place was rendered particularly unhappy by a violent attack of fever. In this forlorn situation I had neither the comfort of medical assistance nor had I medicines to use. The courier returned to Yambo on 19th October with the unpleasant intelligence of Mr. Salt's absence from Cairo, but as this man was the bearer of letters from His Highness Muhumud Ali Pacha to His Excellency Ibrahim Pacha, who had been for some time at Jeddah, I determined to embark on the first boat I could procure and proceed to Jeddah, which place I reached in an open boat in four days.

Although I arrived early on the forenoon of 27th, I was unable to procure any accommodation on shore till the afternoon of the following day. His Excellency's attention was so occupied with the affairs of the Government of his Pashalick, that I experienced considerable difficulty in obtaining an interview, at which the Pacha informed me that he would be at leisure at a future period to converse on the subject of the reply. I ventured to urge a request that he would nominate any of his Ministers or officers through whom I may communicate, but to this request he did not appear to attend.

At my second interview, after a lapse of many days, His Excellency expressed his regret at the delay, which he said had originated in his not being able to procure a scribe capable of drawing up an Arabic letter, but that he would order further inquiry; and that he purposed to draw up a letter, expressing his regret that the communication had not been made at an earlier period, which would have enabled him to unite in the views of the British Government.

His Excellency expressed a wish to send an Arab horse and mare, requesting me to take charge of them, and be the medium of presenting them to the Most Noble the Governor General, to which I of course assented. His Excellency then expressed his intention of conferring a mark of favour on me, and said he should also send a horse for my acceptance, for which I returned my acknowledgments to His Excellency, who informed me that he had ordered a boat (buggalo) to be in readiness to convey me to Mocha.

As it was necessary that I should be acquainted with the reply of His Excellency, I requested that I might be favored with a copy, which may become necessary in the event of accident, and in order to enable me to form a translation, to which His Excellency gave his consent.

On 14th November the draft of the letter was sent to me, with a request that I would return it after perusal, and send the title and address of the Most Noble the Governor General. I complied by transmitting a copy from the letter in my possession in which the title Ushruf-ul-Ushruf, forms a part. To this a very serious objection was stated, as appertaining solely to the Mahomedan Prophet. To obviate difficulties, and prevent cavil as to words, I remarked to the person who was sent to point out the objection, that the title Umjud-ul-Umjud may be easily substituted. His Excellency canvassed this subject with much more warmth than good sense. To me the expression appeared inoffensive. The title of His Highness Abbass Meerza is nearly the same, Nuwab-i-Ushruf, and the different modes of this root are used in a variety of forms to express nobility and pre-eminence in the system of letter-writing in vogue throughout the East, as well in the Arabic as the Persian language. His Excellency and his advisers argued on this point with each other, till religious frenzy gained the ascendancy over their understandings. In this case all cavil and objections were obviated by the proposal of the introduction of an epithet conveying the same sense.

A visit from three or four of His Excellency's Saisés, who came to request a present or donation, was the only further intimation that reached me respecting the horses which His Excellency had directed to be embarked on the boat in which it was intended I should proceed to Mocha. In this instance he had studiously avoided to do me the honour, or pay me the compliment of permitting me to see the animals which he had specially requested me to be the medium of presenting, and regarding which he had consulted with me at the last interview, but on this subject I offered no remark.

One of His Excellency's domestics brought to my residence some parts of a set of horse furniture which he said he had been directed to deliver as an appendage to the horses intended for the Most Noble the Governor General, and that they had been sent in an open or loose state by the Treasurer. These consisted of a headstall, breastplate, and saddle-cloth, silver mounted and gilt, and pair of stirrups of silver. On viewing the saddle cloth it was impossible to avoid observing the tattered condition and ragged appearance which it presented, and which marked it to have been a useful appendage to His Excellency on many former occasions. It did not appear to me that in offering my opinion on a subject on which I had been previously consulted, there could be any risk of offending against the rules of Turkish politeness, and of which I do not propose to plead a total ignorance. I directed the bearer to return in company with the person who was to convey a message to the Chaia on the subject, informing that Minister, that I deferred the acceptance of the saddle furniture, till I should have an opportunity of conversing with him on the subject, and for which purpose I requested to be informed when and where I should have the honour of waiting on him. On the return of His Excellency's messenger the articles were given to him to be conveyed to the Treasurer, till an explanation with the Chaia should take place. As the Chaia did not inform me when he would be at leisure to receive me, I had no opportunity of conversing with him.

His Excellency's Hukeem Bashee, who generally acted as interpreter, was then called upon to discover the motive or grounds for my offering an objection. I acquainted that gentleman with the circumstances, and requested him to convey to His Excellency my readiness to wait on him, and offer my explanations personally. His Excellency preferred an explanation through the interpreter, and I offered the following:—" That the trappings were not a necessary accompaniment, and as they could not be procured in a new or fresh state, it was more politic they should be dispensed with." I authorized the interpreter in the event of His Excellency requiring a further explanation, to offer my opinion, " That articles which had been used could not be considered a suitable present to a nobleman filling so high an official situation under the British Government as the Marquis of Hastings now fills."

His Excellency directed the Hukeem Bashee to convey the following message to me : " That as I had offered an objection on the subject of the trappings, His Excellency had ordered the horses to be disembarked, that the reply was annulled, and the letters ordered to be destroyed, and that His Excellency directed me to depart on the morrow in the boat which had been prepared to convey me to Mocha; that His Excellency on arriving at Cairo would address a letter to the Most Noble the Governor General, returning the sword which had been presented."

To this message there remained only one reply to offer—" That under any other circumstances I should have accepted the accommodation of the buggalow; that I should now procure a vessel at my own expense to convey me to the destination I may now prefer, and at such time as would best suit my convenience."

His Excellency sailed from Jeddah direct for Cossair on 17th November, which circumstance appears at variance with the former arrangement he had made with me of returning *viâ* Yambo, where, had I awaited him, I should probably have avoided the mortification of witnessing the extraordinary alteration which had taken place in His Excellency's deportment from the moment he discovered that the object of this mission could not be converted to his private advantage.

It has unluckily fallen to my lot to have become acquainted with a leading feature of Ibrahim Pacha's character, from personal observation, to which I have to add that the general history of the late campaign entrusted to his management exhibits a series of the most barbarous cruelties, committed in violation of the faith of the most sacred promises; on some occasions to enrich himself by the plunder of the very tribes who had contributed to his successes, and in other cases to obtain possession of the wealth of such of his vanquished enemies as had for a moment screened themselves from his rage. These unfortunate wretches, deluded by the fairest promises, have frequently fallen victims to his avaricious disposition, and insatiable desire to shed human blood.

I have the honour to acquaint your Honourable Board that I have laid before Mr. Salt the particulars of these occurrences, under an impression that His Highness the Viceroy may view the conduct of his son and General in the light it deserves, and may feel inclined to express his disapprobation in such terms as will anticipate the remonstrances which that line of conduct must naturally draw forth; my stay at Jeddah will therefore be deferred till such time as I may receive an answer from Egypt, or hear of the arrival of a vessel from India, which latter circumstance is hardly to be expected at this season.

I have the honour to be, &c.

Jeddah, 18*th November* 1819.

www.ingramcontent.com/pod-product-compliance
Lightning Source LLC
LaVergne TN
LVHW061215060426
835507LV00016B/1937